Psychic Abilities:

Improve your psychic abilities such clairvoyance, telepathy, intuition, aura reading. Increase your mind power and connect to your spirit guide

© Copyright 2020 – CRYSTAL STONES – All rights reserved.

The content contained within this book may not be reproduced, duplicated or transmitted without direct written permission from the author or the publisher.

Under no circumstances will any blame or legal responsibility be held against the publisher, or author, for any damages, reparation, or monetary loss due to the information contained within this book. Either directly or indirectly.

Legal Notice:

This book is copyright protected. This book is only for personal use. You cannot amend, distribute, sell, use, quote or paraphrase any part, or the content within this book, without the consent of the author or publisher.

Disclaimer Notice:

Please note the information contained within this document is for educational and entertainment purposes only. All effort has been executed to present accurate, up to date, and reliable, complete information. No warranties of any kind are declared or implied. Readers acknowledge that the author is not engaging in the rendering of legal, financial, medical or professional advice. The content within this book has been derived from various sources. Please consult a licensed professional before attempting any techniques outlined in this book.

By reading this document, the reader agrees that under no circumstances is the author responsible for any losses, direct or indirect, which are incurred as a result of the use of information contained within this document, including, but not limited to, — errors, omissions, or inaccuracies.

TABLE OF CONTENS

INTRODUCTION 1
THE HISTORY OF PSYCHICS 7
EARLY SIGNS AND TYPES OF PSYCHIC ABILITIES .. 14
SIGNS YOU MAY ALREADY HAVE PSYCHIC ABILITIES 21
PREDISPOSITION OF PSYCHIC ABILITIES 35
WHAT IS PSYCHIC POWER AND HOW DO YOU DISCOVER YOUR INTUITIVE TYPE? 41
THE ART OF CRYSTAL GAZING OR SCRYING 56
EVALUATING PSYCHIC EXPERIENCES 72
A SHORT HISTORY OF PSYCHIC & PARANORMAL ABILITIES 89
THE INTUITION 97
THE LANGUAGE OF DIVINATION 103
THE FIRST STEP TO DEVELOPING YOUR PSYCHIC POWER 114
PROTECTING YOURSELF AGAINST SPIRITS 120
CONCLUSION 127

Introduction

What Does It Mean to Be a Psychic?

When we speak of being psychic, we mean accepting information via more inputs than just the five distinct senses. Extrasensory perception is a capability we all can learn to use. Think of it as a graded distinction from a strong taste, sight, sound, smell, or touch which you can identify and describe; to something fainter, that you might just barely remember; to information you might only fully understand having received after years of analysis. This last might be described as "sub-sensory perception", and then the next level concerns perceptions that cannot be explained by our known physical capabilities. We tend to describe these perceptions in spiritual terms because we are, so far, unable to fully understand or examine what they are, what makes them happen, or what we can do with them.

Since we don't know how, when, or why psychic abilities will manifest, we tend to react to them with fear. This reaction is compounded by a defensive reflex against anyone knowing more about us than we want them to. When we think someone is using an unfair advantage to achieve greater success than our own, we also have a tendency to feel threatened and attempt to suppress that person's advantage. These are common reactions among people from all walks of life. Even unusual knowledge or skill in matters that can be readily explained, can raise suspicion and hostility. Sadly, unscrupulous people press every advantage, thus many gifted abilities have unfortunately earned a distrusted reputation.

If psychic ability means receiving information from sources we can't explain, then we all have it. Some people receive more frequent and distinct perceptions than others. Some people find it very difficult to believe in anything they can't explore with all five familiar senses. It is possible to open ourselves to more information, and learn to increase our reliance on what we tell ourselves. As we proceed, we will investigate methods and practices for increasing this openness and self-trust. We will study how to recognize different ways by which we try to shortcut our conscious judgment with important information.

In two well publicized examples, a wildlife photographer experienced sudden terror while setting up his equipment. Unable to overcome the compulsion, he abandoned his equipment and fled, for no reason he could explain. His actions made more sense to him when he returned after some short time and reviewed the footage of a leopard investigating his camera a few minutes after his departure.

In another situation, a woman felt a sudden surge of fear she could neither explain nor ignore, and surprised herself by taking bold action. It was only later that she learned that she had saved her own life, and by diligent review pieced together the clues she had unconsciously connected. Both of these stories can be explained by what these people saw, heard, or potentially smelled, but the point is that they didn't know that at the time. A great deal of the development of psychic ability is accepting that you know more than you can process with your rational mind.

B. Nine Categories of Psychic Abilities

Potentially psychic experiences are frequently written off as coincidence, or forgotten about as if they were both too uncomfortable and inexplicable to have been real. For some people, psychic ability is so deeply associated with scary monsters that they fear to acknowledge their own experiences. If we imagine, for instance, that the psychic senses might be possible effects of brain synapse connections we haven't yet mapped, it makes more sense that these experiences would be as common as they are. There is nothing inherently frightening about any of these experiences, and they have not been documented to have directly injured their participants. It is very likely that every reader will have experienced at least one of the following possible indicators of psychic ability.

1. Visions

Psychic visions may interrupt what we are doing to an inconvenient extent, and hallucinations are a common enough effect of dangerous medical conditions that the experience may be frightening. Make your health the priority, but there is no need to fear the experience of altered perception as long as safety precautions are observed. Sometimes psychic potential is opened due to a medical condition, and many patients celebrate this development while working with doctors to manage their physical needs.

2. Hearing Sounds

Sometimes a friend's voice calls your name. Another time, you may be sitting in a quiet room and hear a bell ring, or a crowd of children shouting. You may hear murmuring, or a single voice speaking quite clearly. As with visions, this can be one of the frightening manifestations of psychic ability, in part because it may interfere with day-to-day activities, and in part because the experiences are often symptoms of medical conditions. If you have any concerns about possible symptoms of illness or injury, always discuss them with a medical professional, but there is no reason to be afraid of the manifestations themselves.

3. Strong Intuition

This may be described as reliably lucky guesses. If you can call a coin flip or a roulette wheel; if you know who is calling just before the phone rings, if you have ever been in a crowd and known what people would do before they did, you have very strong intuition.

4. Déjà vu

If you have ever felt as though you are repeating a moment you already lived, it is called déjà vu, ("previously seen" in French), and may indicate a level of psychic talent. This may also present as knowledge of the layout of a place you've never been, or a sense of knowing the destined conclusion of a series of events.

5. Premonition

If you can describe future events, that is a very potent psychic ability. Make a practice of writing down what you think is going to happen. If you have these predictions, and they come true, that's probably a sign that you have unusual psychic strength.

6. Dreams

Most dreams are the brain making stories as it processes the day's information. These stories might be vivid, detailed, and full of symbols and layers of meaning. Some dreams may be powerful psychic communication. Paying attention to your dreams and learning to remember them is one way to increase your psychic access.

7. Telepathic Connection

Telepathy means you are involved with the thoughts and feelings of other people. You may be highly sensitive to others' emotions, or even hear their thoughts. This ability is important to regulate skillfully, because people can often sense intrusions of this nature and react with hostility.

8. Sensing Danger

Sometimes you may be flooded with dread for the safety of a loved one. This may be an immediate situation, or a more remote foreboding. Especially if you do not usually feel anxious about the person or situation, this can be real information. Remember, one possible source of knowledge we can't explain is the subconscious mind, where the brain interprets cues from the environment at the speed of electricity. We don't want to be ruled by fear, but we should never automatically rule out our fears, either. Whenever someone's sense of danger is alerted, they should take it seriously.

9.Psychic Travel

If you have ever had an out-of-body experience, seen visions of a place you weren't located, or had a dream in which you experienced travel or transport to a different place, you may be able to learn astral projection.

The History Of Psychics

Some of the first evidence of psychics dates back to the Roman Empire. At the time, they were referred to as clairvoyants and worked as advisors. It is said that the psychics had a direct connection to the gods and goddesses. They would communicate to them and inform the kings and queens about their messages. Psychics were a big part of the decision-making process. They were consulted for every decision, no matter how big or small. This included the decision to go to war, to harvest and plant crops, and take government action. Sadly, this also came at a cost. If the decision that was made based on the psychic's opinion failed, the psychic would often be jailed or sentenced to death.

A psychic's role progressed as civilization progressed. When tribes began to form, shamans possessed psychic abilities. They became the primary doctors of villages. Once again, shamans played a very important role in the society. They were always present at ceremonies to provide cosmic energy. They would perform divination—the practice of seeing the future or answering questions—using clairvoyance or out-of-body experiences.

Eventually, psychics began to use objects to promote the conjuring of spiritual energy. When a psychic had advanced their powers, they would start to use tools such as jewels, crystals, bones, and divining rods. They could use them to encourage greater energy. Dice and dominoes are now accepted as effective tools for advanced psychic readings.

Psychics also developed the theory of luck. They explained that there isn't good luck or bad luck; it is all just energy. The energy around you controls the outcome in some situations. Most people are not aware of the type of energy they are releasing into the universe. This energy ends up reflecting back on them, either positively or negatively. This is an important reason why you must learn to understand and control your abilities.

With the rise of organized religious society, the acceptance of psychic ability disappeared. Jewish, Christian, and Islamic leaders all proclaimed that psychics were nothing more than witches or evil beings. Religious leaders began to fear that the ability to foretell would cause them to lose control of their congregations. Foretelling, similar to psychic intuition, is the ability to sense what is going to happen. Religious leaders feared they would no longer be seen as the people with connections to higher beings. This led to psychics being banished, sent to jail, or killed.

One of the most famous historical stories of psychics is the Salem Witch Trials. From February 1692 to May 1693, a group of girls convinced an entire village that many of its citizens were witches. It began with Betty Parris, 9, and Abigail Williams, 11, experiencing "fits" that they blamed on witchcraft. Women and men were sentenced to death for their supposed work with the devil. In all, 19 people were hanged, many of them women. One 71-year-old man was pressed to death, and several people died in jail, two of whom were infants. Nearly 200 people were accused of being witches. The Christian church helped lead the Salem Witch Trials because it felt that psychic ability was an insult to their creator. Luckily, a new court was put into place and almost everybody had their charges absolved and got back their good names.

Fortunately, now psychics are an accepted part of society. That's not to say there aren't people who still don't believe in such a thing. Police departments are now employing psychics to help them solve crimes. Scientific research has shown that psychic abilities are real, and are now an area of study. Research has shown that psychic abilities are like the energy observed in quantum physics. Psychics have even made it onto TV shows as main characters, and it's hard not to find a book on the subject.

Religious leaders still disapprove of psychic abilities. They still warn their flocks about the evil doings of psychics, writing them off as frauds, con artists, or devil worshipers. Despite the growing amount of evidence that such abilities do exist, psychics remain unwanted guests in many religious institutions.

Psychic Intuition

Intuition is the feeling of being pulled in a certain direction, which normally can't be explained. Most of the time, people refer to this as a gut instinct, just like when you meet someone new and get a feeling about whether you will like them. You can also look at it as your inner voice or higher self that is connected to something bigger in the universe. When you can quiet your mind, your voice will become clearer and louder. Being psychic is having more detailed intuitive information. It helps build more from your intuition, making it clearer and giving you more insight. The information you receive can be through clairvoyance, clairaudience, clairsentience, claircognizance, or clairgustance.

Instead of getting a gut feeling about whether you will like a person, you will get a picture or know a detail from their life.

The first of the four main intuitive abilities is clairvoyance, meaning clear seeing. It is the most common type of psychic intuition. Clairvoyance is the ability to see something in your mind's eye. It's like seeing a movie inside your head. It doesn't mean you are seeing the future or something major; it can sometimes be subtle. You might see only a color, a number, or a symbol. It will be up to you to figure out what they mean but they can be full-blown premonitions.

The second ability is clairsentience, which means clear feeling. Clairsentience means you can receive intuitive messages by feelings, emotions, or sensations. Empathy is a common form of clairsentience. These types of people often find themselves feeling extremely drained because they are constantly bombarded by negative and positive feelings and emotions. You may walk up to somebody you barely know and realize exactly how they feel. Clairsentience also gives you the ability to know if someone is lying to you, which can come in handy. If your abilities are very strong, you may even start to feel sick when others close to you are ill.

The third ability is clairaudience, which means clear hearing. It's a way to receive messages without using your physical ear. Just like clairvoyance is inner seeing, clairaudience is inner hearing. Maybe you have heard somebody tell you something but nobody is around you, or the person you are with didn't say anything. Psychics will hear a spirit speaking to them in their heads. It will sound like when you are reading silently to yourself. On some occasions, they may hear the voice in the accent of the person talking to them.

The fourth ability is claircognizance, which means clear knowing. This is the ability to know something without having information or facts. You may simply know that you shouldn't trust your new neighbor or a person who just started working in your office. These feelings can be extremely strong and pop into your head at random times. You may have had some of these thoughts before. Maybe you were getting ready to get on the elevator but a thought popped into your head and told you to take the stairs. Then you found out later that the elevator had gotten stuck.

One of the less common and less-known psychic intuitions is clairalience, which is clear smelling. This is the ability to smell beyond the normal aptitude. An example is if you're at home and smell perfume, a cigar, or any smell you associate with a deceased relative. Another less common ability is clairgustance, which means clear tasting. This is the ability to taste something before you put it in your mouth. It is usually experienced by mediums during a reading. When a psychic is trying to communicate with an entity, they can start developing a taste in their mouth. For example, if the entity they are trying to reach liked chocolate when they were alive, the psychic might begin to taste chocolate.

These are a few examples of psychic intuition. You do not have to maintain all these abilities. You may have only one or two, and you may end up having all of them at various times depending on how an entity wants to communicate with you.

Early Signs And Types Of Psychic Abilities

Psychic ability doesn't play favorites. It's not something only certain people can have. There is a wide range of strength in terms of a person's psychic ability. This could mean that you have anything from a feeling that someone is going to call you to an ability to read other people's emotions and thoughts. Research has shown that everybody is born able to develop psychic abilities. Researchers have also found that ancestry and childhood play a large role in whether the ability develops on its own or whether one must develop their own.

Ancestry

It's believed that one's family history plays a large role in determining whether a child is more prone to being psychic. To add to this, during the time when villages used shamans, the shaman's child would be trained to take over after his father's death. Another example of families playing a big part in psychic ability is sisters Kate and Maggie Fox, who worked together to found Spiritualism. They were both advanced psychics. Spiritualism is communication with the spirits of the dead.

A study in Scotland led by Shari Cohn started studying the patterns among families in the Highlands and Western Isles of Scotland. She noticed that many of the families seemed to have the abilities of second sight (which is being able to see events in remote places where the psychic is not present), retro-cognition (seeing the past), and precognition (seeing the future). Two hundred and eight people were studied and Cohn found that a large percentage of the population possessed psychic abilities. She also confirmed that women were more likely to be psychic, and if a person had a twin, or had twins in their family, they were more likely to be psychic.

Additionally, Cohn's research showed that families that had psychic abilities and believed in them, encouraging their use, had a long line of psychics. Sylvia Wright also confirmed this relation. In households where psychic abilities are not believed in or supported by the family, children usually repress their skills, whereas children with families that support and encourage them will have strong psychic abilities.

One psychic spoke with a sociologist and, during their interview, told them how one night when she was a child, she told her mother that a man was standing in the corner of her room. Her mother replied by asking, "What is his name?"

In another story, a psychic told how her grandmother used to help her strengthen her ability with games, including hiding a key in her house and telling her to "be the key, then see where you are."

Damaging Childhood

Stress and trauma experienced in childhood are other strong factors in developing psychic ability. A researcher who had interviewed several psychics and mediums over several years said that almost every person interviewed had experienced some sort of personal trauma in their childhoods. The University of Chicago found similar results while interviewing psychics. Its study showed that children who experienced tension in their families or who had a difficult relationship with a parent (the father more so than the mother) were more likely to develop psychic ability. Interestingly, these subjects had an above-average score for their current life satisfaction. The conclusion was that psychic abilities had a correlation to difficult upbringings, but didn't affect happiness in adult life.

Science explains this as "use it or lose it." We are born with hundreds of thousands of brain cells. As we grow up, if these cells are not used, they will die off. What you experience during childhood dictates what brain cells will be kept, normally before the age of 10. The brain's organization is controlled by the way the cells develop. If a child shows psychic abilities, encouraging them will tell the brain to continue using those brain cells, allowing the child's abilities to grow. Not using them will cause those cells to die off.

Proteins are produced when genes are allowed to be expressed, which in turn develops genes, cells, and neurons. When a child who has a predisposition toward being a psychic is supported and helped to improve their psychic abilities, more pathways are created in the brain, allowing for further development. Genes that support psychic abilities are found primarily in the prefrontal cortex. The cortex will continue to grow in supported, intelligent children until around the age of 11 or 12.

Psychologists have studied the reasoning behind psychic ability due to trauma. They say that when children are put in a traumatic situation, the brain normally disassociates from its surroundings. For protection, it will divert the child away from conscious reality. Disassociating allows the brain to tune into other realities, possibly even other worlds, places, and times. In some studies, adults who had experienced traumatic events as children recalled having out-of-body experiences. One such psychic said that physical abuse occurred almost daily. She said that during the abuse, she wouldn't hear or feel anything, even though she knew and could see what was happening. She would become numb to escape.

Another study explaining childhood stress-induced psychic ability looked at children of alcoholics or drug addicts. AL-ANON is a group for adult children of addicts. The group often talks about the perception of others' feelings, usually parents. One participant, during a study in 1999, said that many times he would arrive home not knowing whether his mother was passed out somewhere. As he walked into the house, before he ever saw her, he could tell what his mother's current state was. He unconsciously trained himself to read her mind and moods so that he would know when she was more likely to become irrational and unstable. This is known as being a psychic empath—being able to feel the pain and emotions of others. Instead of disassociation, children who develop this do so as a means of self-preservation.

Some other predictors for psychic abilities are if a child was raised by authoritarian, strict, or abusive parents, such as unloving parents who forced and demanded total obedience. Other predictors are if a toddler lost their mother, had an extreme sickness or deformity that required a number of corrective surgeries or had parents who both suffered from bi-polar disorder. The chance of having psychic ability is heightened with a combination of stressors and family history.

Studies show that everybody is born with the possibility to possess psychic tendencies, but they usually require a trigger, like childhood trauma, a stressor, or family history. This usually must happen before age 10 for the frontal lobe to thicken, allowing synapses and neurons to form. An exception is if the child is extremely intelligent, possessing a high IQ; in this case, they have until the age of 12 for the frontal lobe changes to take place. There are more psychic women who came from families' rich with psychic abilities or multiple births. Males who had a generally happy upbringing, no history of multiple births, or no family history of psychic abilities or beliefs are least likely to develop abilities.

Think back to when you were a child. How was it? Did you experience a lot of stressors growing up? Did a parent die when you were young? Did you ever have strange moments when you sensed something was about to happen or saw things others couldn't? Maybe you were raised in a family that nurtured your gift. Now you're looking for a way to nurture it, even more, to enhance your life and learn how you can live better with psychic abilities. If any of these sounds familiar, you have chosen the right book.

Signs You May Already Have Psychic Abilities

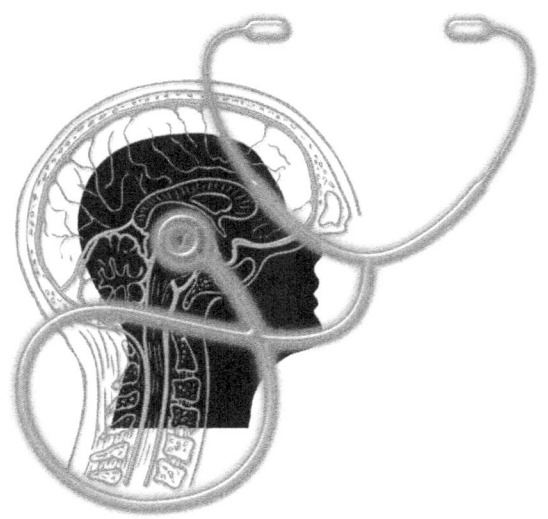

Have you ever had the feeling that you already have some psychic skills or abilities? Perhaps you have plenty of experiences with déjàvu that you don't believe are significant, or you think that each time you accurately predict something, it's a mere coincidence. Are you guilty of ignoring unusual events that happen to you, or do you actually pause to look deeply? Many of us who already have psychic skills in one way or another do not recognize them for what they are, and so they go unused or worse, unnoticed. Recognizing the skills that you may already have is crucial for this path.

Why do People Ignore their Psychic Abilities?

- Afraid to be seen as "Weird": Our world does not always glorify or praise higher seeing, which may lead some people to hold back their abilities out of fear of being seen as different or weird. People do not always appreciate it when others see more than they do, and may resent someone who sees deeply into reality and is open about it. When you don't have friends around who understand this interest of yours, it can be hard to listen to your intuition or stay faithful to your path.

- Psychics are, at Times, seen as "Evil": At times, people with psychic abilities are even seen as witches, evil, or interested in the black arts, which is not necessarily true at all. As mentioned earlier, everyone has these abilities, but most aren't aware of how to see them for what they are, haven't noticed them, or simply ignore them on purpose. However, some people may call these abilities evil, which will lead some to hide their skills. It's important to remember that these skills are not evil at all and are just a natural part of being a human.

It's also possible that the person with psychic abilities may be called crazy or nonsensical if they are open about their skills or use them in front of others. It's a shame that we live in a world that downplays such an important and natural gift, but being aware of some of the stigma against these abilities can help you move past being held back by it. Once you develop along your psychic path, these judgments from others will not matter to you as much.

Signs that you have Psychic Skills:

For someone who naturally has these abilities in a large amount, they can only be held back for so long before they come out. Read over some of these signs and symptoms that might mean you already have some of these abilities. Perhaps you will realize that you're already halfway there, and only need to know what you should be looking for. Once you are aware of what these skills look like, you can move onto developing them even further, or choosing which you want to focus on. Do any of these descriptions fit you?

- Higher than Average Intuitive Abilities: Have you heard the phone ring and already knew who it was, before seeing their name on the caller ID? Perhaps you can sense it when a text message is about to be sent to you, or have known an event was coming before anyone else. If you have the ability to sense whether someone has good or bad energy from across the room, before even speaking with them, you have highly developed intuition. This is, as mentioned earlier, the first step on the journey of uncovering all of your psychic abilities.

- Visions Occur Regularly to you: For someone with psychic abilities, visions can be quite normal and occur often. If you've envisioned the future on multiple occasions, whether in dreams or waking life, you definitely have some level of psychic skill. These visions may depict what is happening in the next hour, or the next few months, and are significant at times, and seemingly trivial at others. In order to test this, start noting down your visions and ideas of what is going to happen, to see if you can confirm them later on.

- Déjàvu is Normal to you: Déjàvu is something that everyone has experienced at least once, but for someone with higher than average psychic abilities, it's a common occurrence. If you always feel as though you've seen this place before when you really haven't, or sense familiarity in new things, places, or people, you are probably going through déjàvu. This is a signal that your psychic abilities are already in tune. Once your psychic abilities are heightened even more, this might become an everyday occurrence for you.

- Accurate Gut Feelings on a Regular Basis: For someone with psychic abilities, knowing what will happen before it does, is natural. You may be able to tell how events will play out, even if it's just a general sense of "good" or "bad". You may even be able to sense when you are going to get along well or badly with someone just from looking at them, or in extreme cases, sense when a natural disaster is about to hit across the world.

- Occurrences of Telepathy: Have you ever felt as though your mind can send messages to other people? Have you picked up the thoughts or emotions of others seemingly without any effort? Perhaps you have noticed that you are having a connection with someone else without even saying one word, or have engaged in a full conversation with someone without talking at all. These are all signs of being psychic, and skills that can be strengthened with effort and practice.

- Vivid Dreaming: When someone has psychic skills, they often also have a tendency to experience vivid dreams, which they can recall even after waking up, in detail. They see symbols in these vivid dreams that can show deep metaphorical significance to the dreamer, and also show hidden messages that pertain to what is happening in their life at the time. A lot of people even have dreams that recur and tell a story that is hidden within the subconscious mind. Tapping into this skill can lend valuable insights to your own mind.

- Sensing History of Objects or People: Being able to sense the history of an object or person after touching it or them is another psychic skill that you may naturally possess. One way in which psychics are so powerful is because they are able to sense facts about objects, places, or people by simply focusing. They sometimes are able to hug someone or hold their hand and suddenly experience or sense pieces of that person's past.

- Premonitions and Predictions: If you've ever recorded thoughts down because you knew they were going to occur later on, and then seen them happen, this is quite obviously proof of a latent psychic ability. You could have known they were coming from a dream you had, or simply a feeling that appeared to come out of nowhere.

- You know when Trouble is Coming: There is a strong feeling that happens when someone senses their loved one in danger. This can cause you to panic for no apparent or immediate reason, and cause a huge impact on you. There might be no instant explanation for this feeling, other than the overwhelming sense that someone close to you is in trouble. In some cases, you might know who it is specifically, while for others, you will simply know it's someone close to you.

- You feel Events from Far Away: This ability is quite advanced and tells you that you are definitely psychic. Perhaps once you were either at work or at home, and could sense something happening from far away, either in another city or even country. If you've felt experiences from across the globe and knew what was going on, right as it happened, you likely have very advanced psychic skills. This could have been anything from a detailed, clear vision, to a strong sense of trouble happening somewhere specific.

- You have Healing Abilities: Some psychic people are able to touch someone ill or suffering and notice that they feel better almost instantly. Someone with psychic gifts has strong and usually positive energy that can be used to heal either mental or physical wounds in other people. If this has happened to you, it's likely the cause of your psychic abilities.

- You Predict Future Events: This one is quite obvious, but being able to predict future events, telling them to someone close to you, then seeing the event actually occur, is one main way to tell that you have psychic abilities. These intuitions often come at the most unexpected of times, and often without rhyme or reason, until the event occurs and makes it clear for you.

- Having Access to Sounds: Hearing sounds when no one else can, and always wondering why nobody is reacting to those subtle chimes or rings, can tell you that you have latent psychic skills. These noises might be pointing to an event that is yet to come. Some people with this skill are been able to narrow down what each sound means and use it to their advantage, or to help other people.

Possessing psychic abilities need not make you afraid or anxious. These skills are wonderful gifts and, when developed fully, can be used in extraordinary ways. Psychic people are very helpful and valuable to others that have yet to notice or harness their own skills in this arena. People tend to trust those with psychic abilities, even if they aren't sure why they trust them. This can be for multiple reasons, from guidance, to support, to solving mysteries, or even a simple intuitive pull. When you learn to embrace these skills as blessings from nature, you can begin to put them toward helping the world.

A Psychic History

The first evidence of physics goes all the way back to the Roman Empire. These people were called clairvoyants and would work as advisors. Everyone thought they had direct connections to the goddesses and gods. The psychics would communicate with the gods and give the Royalty messages. Psychics were used to make important decisions. They were consulted about each decision. It didn't matter how minute or large. These decisions could be about going to war, government actions, and planting and harvesting their crops. All of this came with a cost. If royalty made a decision based on the psychic's advice, and that decision turned out badly, the psychic could be jailed or killed.

The role of psychics grew with the progression of civilization. When tribes formed, Shaman had the psychic abilities. They were the doctors for the village. The shaman had an important role in their society. They were at every ceremony to give cosmic energy. They performed divination, which means they would look into the future for answers, but using out-of-body experiences or clairvoyance.

Psychics started using objects to help them conjure up spiritual energy. When their powers had advanced, they would use tools like bones, jewels, crystals, and divining rods. These items were used to encourage greater energy. Dice and dominoes are accepted to be tools for advanced psychic readings.

Psychics developed the theory of luck. They informed that there is not good or bad luck, it is all energy. This energy is always around you and can control the outcome of certain situations. Most aren't aware of the energy they release into the world. This energy will get reflected back to them in either a positive or negative way. This is why you must learn to control and understand your abilities.

When organized religion gained popularity, they no longer accepted psychic abilities. Christian, Jewish, and Islamic leaders deemed psychics were evil beings, Satan worshippers, or witches. Religious leaders feared their ability of foretelling and thought it would cause people to stop coming to services. Foretelling is similar to psychic intuition and is the ability to sense that something is going to happen. The religious leaders thought they would be looked at as not having connections to higher beings. This caused psychics to be jailed, banished, or killed.

The most famous historical story of psychics is the Salem Witch Trials. This took place between February 1692 and May 1693. A group of young girls convinced their whole village that many of their inhabitants were witches. It began simply enough with Betty Parris who was nine and Abigail Williams who was 11. They began to experience "fits" in which they claimed were caused by witchcraft. Both women and men were killed for their so-called work with Satan. One man who was 71-years old was pressed to death. Several died in jail two of these fatalities were infants.

Nineteen people were hung. Many were women. Around 200 people were accused of being witches. The Salem Witch Trials were led by The Christian Church because they thought psychic abilities was insulting to their creator. A new court was created, and almost everyone got their sentenced absolved and their good name back.

Psychics are a normal part of our society today. That's not saying there aren't people out there who do not believe in this sort of thing. Police departments have used psychics to help solve cold cases and abductions. Research has shown that psychics are real and are an accepted area of study. Studies have shown that psychic abilities are similar to the energy in quantum physics. Psychics can be seen on many TV shows as the main character. You can find many books out there on this subject.

Religious leaders still disprove psychic abilities. They always warn their parishioners about the evils of psychics. They write them off as frauds, devil worshippers, or con artists. In spite of huge amounts of evidence that these abilities do exist, psychics still remain as unwanted guests in most religious institutions.

Intuition

Intuition is feeling like you are being pulled to do something specific that can't be explained. Most people call this a gut instinct. You might have met someone and instantly know whether or not you were going to like them. This can also be thought of as an inner voice or higher self that connects you to something much bigger in the galaxy. If you can calm your mind, this voice can become louder and clearer.

Psychic abilities go into more detailed information. It can help your intuition to build more from what you are feeling to make things clearer and give you better insight. This information can be brought through clairaudience, clairvoyance, clairsentience, clairgustance, or claircognizance. Instead of that gut feeling about not liking someone, you will either know something specific or see something specific about their past.

The first of the many intuitive abilities is clairaudience. This means clear hearing. You receive messages without using your actual ears. Clairaudience is inner hearing. You might have had someone tell you something, but no one is around you, or the person you are standing next to didn't say anything. Psychics can hear spirits talk to them. It will be like you are reading to yourself. Sometimes, you might hear a voice in the accent of the person who is talking through them.

The second is clairvoyance. This means clear seeing. This is the most common intuition. Clairvoyance is being able to see something with your mind's eye. To simplify, it is like watching a movie in your head. This does not mean they are looking into the future or anything major; it is usually subtle. You could just see a number, color, or symbol. You will have to figure out what it means. It might actually be a premonition.

The third is clairsentience. This means clear feeling. This means you get messages through emotions, feelings, and sensations. Empathy is the most common form. People who are empaths usually feel drained since they are always bombarded by both negative and positive emotions and feelings. You might walk up to someone you just barely know and can "feel" exactly what they are feeling. It gives you an ability to know if someone is lying. This is very handy. If your abilities are extremely strong, you might begin to feel sick when you are around a lot of people with bad energy.

The fourth is clairgustance. This means clear tasting. With this, you can taste something before ever putting it into your mouth. Mediums sometimes experience this during a reading. When psychics try to communicate with others, they might begin to develop a taste in their mouths. If the person they are trying to reach liked chocolate, they the psychic might actually taste chocolate.

The fifth is claircognizance. This is clear knowing. This ability allows you to know something without seeing any facts or information. You might just know that you can't trust your neighbor or that new person you just started working with. These feelings might be strong and just pop in your head at any time. You might have had some similar thoughts before. You might have been standing and waiting for an elevator, but something just told you to take the stairs. When you get to the floor you wanted, you find out the elevator got stuck between floors.

A lesser common intuition is clairalience. This is clear smelling. This gives you the ability to smell beyond your normal ability. If you have ever been sitting, reading a book, relaxing in your favorite chair and got a strong odor of a cigar, pipe, perfume, or any smell you can associate with a deceased relative.

These are just examples of different intuitions. You do not have to have all of them. You might only have one or two, or you could experience all of them at one point in your life. It all depends on how a person wants to communicate with you.

Predisposition of Psychic Abilities

Psychic abilities will not play favorites. It isn't something that certain people get. The strength of a person's ability has a wide range. This means that you might get a feeling that someone is trying to call you. You could start to be able to read other's thoughts and emotions. Studies have shown that every person is born with the ability to develop their psychic abilities. Ancestry and childhood also play huge roles in whether or not the ability develops by itself or if a person must develop it on their own.

Ancestry

A person's family history can play a huge role in whether a child is prone to become a psychic. During the time of Shamans, a Shaman's child would get trained to take over after their father's death. For another example of family playing roles in psychic abilities, sisters Maggie and Kate Fox founded Spiritualism together. They were both very advanced psychics. Spiritualism is being able to communicate with dead people's spirits.

Shari Cohn led a study in Scotland to study patterns within families in the Highlands and Western Isles of Scotland. She saw that many families had a second sight ability. They were able to see events in places where they were not at. Some had retrocognition or the ability to see the past. Some showed signs of precognition where they could see into the future. She found that out of the 208 people who were studied, a large part of them did possess a psychic ability. She confirmed that women are more psychic than men. If a person had a twin, or twins ran in the family, they were more prone to be psychic.

Cohn's research also showed that families who had psychic abilities and believed in their abilities and encouraged their use had long lines of psychics in the family. Sylvia Wright has confirmed this relation. In families where psychic abilities aren't supported or believed in, children will repress any skills they possess. Children whose family encourages and supports them show very strong psychic abilities.

A sociologist interviewed a psychic who told her about an event she has as a child. She woke her mom and told her a man was standing in the corner of her room. Her mom replied with, "Did you ask him what his name is?" She didn't discourage her but encouraged her to explore her abilities.

Another psychic recalled how her grandmother helped her strengthen her own abilities. Her grandmother would hide an item somewhere in her house and told her to "be this item, and see where you are."

Childhood Trauma

Trauma that is experienced during childhood helps to develop psychic ability. A researcher interviewed a lot of psychics and medium over numerous years found that each person they interviewed has some type of personal trauma at a young age. The University of Chicago found similar results when they did their interviews of psychics. This study showed children who had tension within the family unit, had problem relationships with their father developed a psychic ability. They had a great score for the satisfaction they felt in life. This showed that psychic abilities did have a relationship with problem upbringings but didn't affect their happiness in adulthood.

Science calls it the "use it or lose it" syndrome. We are born with hundreds and thousands of brain cells. While growing up, if we do not use these cells, they die off. The experiences you have during childhood can dictate what brain cells you keep into adulthood. This will happen before they turn ten years old. How the brain organizes its cells is controlled by how the cells developed. If children show psychic abilities, encouraging them will allow the brain to use those cells. This will help their ability to grow. If they aren't used, they will die.

When genes are expressed, proteins are produced these will turn into genes, cells, and neurons. When a psychic child is supported and helped to improve their abilities, this will make new pathways in the brain and allows for more development. Genes that help psychic abilities are found in the prefrontal cortex. This will grow in children who are intelligent and supported until the age of 12.

Psychologists have studied why trauma causes psychic abilities. When children are forced into a traumatic situation, the brain will disassociate itself from the surroundings. It diverts the child out of the conscious reality to protect them. Disassociation allows the brain to turn to other realities and possibly other worlds, times, and places. Adults who had traumatic childhood events recalled having out of body experiences as children. One psychic recalled that she suffered from physical abuse daily. During these times, she couldn't hear or feel anything. She knew and saw what was happening, but she turned numb to escape the torture.

Another study explained that childhood stress caused psychic abilities talked with children whose parents were drug addicts or alcoholics. AL-ANON is a group for adult children of addicts. This group often talks about other's feelings, usually their parents. One participant said many times he would come home not knowing if his mother would be passed out in the house or not. He stated that he was able to tell what his mother's mood was before he ever saw her. He had unconsciously trained himself to read her moods and mind so he could know when she would be unstable or irrational. He had become an empath. He was able to feel the emotions and pain of others. Instead of disassociation, children developed empathy as a way to self-preserve.

Other predictors for psychic abilities are children who were raised by strict, authoritarian, or abusive parents. Unloving parents who forced and demanded total obedience. If a toddler lost their mother, has a serious sickness or deformity that needed many corrective surgeries, and children whose parents were bi-polar. The chances of developing a psychic ability are greater when there is a combination of different stressors along with family history.

Studies have shown that every person born can possess psychic abilities. They normally require triggers like stressor, childhood trauma, or family history. This will happen before they turn ten so the frontal lobe will thicken and allows synapses and neurons to form. If the child is intelligent and possesses a higher IQ, they will have until the age of 12 before the frontal lobe changes. More women psychics come from families rich in psychic abilities or multiple births. Males who have a happy upbringing, no multiple births, no history of abilities or belief are not as likely to develop any psychic abilities.

Think about your childhood. Was it a good one? Did you experience any stressors? Did you have a parent die when you were very young? Did you have moments when you sensed something was going to happen or see things that others around you couldn't see? You might have been raised in a family that helped you with your gift. Now you want to find a way to nurture it more to help make your life better. Learn how you can live better with your abilities. If this sounds like you, you have chosen the right book.

What Is Psychic Power And How Do You Discover Your Intuitive Type?

Real-life psychic abilities aren't really like what we grew up watching on TV. Psychics don't get a vivid flash into the future out of nowhere, like a little movie playing in their mind's eye, just in time to warn the subject of the vision so that they can change their fate – the ability to sense what the future holds isn't just the stuff of Hollywood. Although it's a lot subtler than how it's portrayed on TV, it's more of a heightened intuition.

Now, everyone has intuition, but some people's psychic intuition is stronger than others for a number of different reasons – the most common being that they don't exercise it much, as they usually don't believe in intuition, and as a result, don't listen to it or can't detect it. It could also be because of emotional blockage or trauma that leaves you unable to tap into your psychic channel and focus your energy properly. Therefore, it never gets developed and lies unused and dormant in a person's subconscious.

See, your intuition is like a muscle – you have to keep using it and practicing with it for it to develop into true psychic ability. If you've grown up in an environment where you were encouraged to trust your "sixth sense" as it were, you are more likely to have stronger psychic ability. But there's good news for those who were brought up by the skeptics of the world and/or if you're a skeptic yourself! Even if you didn't have this early exposure and permission to develop your gift, that doesn't disqualify you from achieving psychic power. For those of you in need of a bit of a spiritual workout, let's get started!

One thing people who are perhaps more in touch with their intuition often find themselves asking when they have a sense something is amiss is: am I just being anxious and paranoid, or is my sense of foreboding legitimate? The trick that usually works for getting to the bottom of doubt about your sense and whether it's just anxiety or an actual premonition is: if you feel a sudden flash of foreboding or some sense that something's going to go wrong and then it disappears – that's your intuition. Heed the feeling and listen to what it's telling you, what it's warning you of. It could be gravely important. However, it won't stay long, so try your best to interpret it while it's there – you can even write down how it feels. If you get a sense that something is wrong and just can't stop thinking about it all day to the point where you're overthinking it and overanalyzing it to try and figure out what it means and how you can solve it to the point that you're quite worked up and that it just won't go away – it's more likely just anxiety and not a true psychic prediction in this case. It's easy to tell when it's anxiety because the feeling just won't leave you alone.

Another sign that it's a psychic premonition would be a type of tingling feeling. Psychic premonitions are also generally accompanied by a feeling of tingling in your brain, usually on top or between your eyes. They don't always come with this feeling, but the chances are if whatever you think you're sensing is accompanied by tingling in your head, then it's fairly safe to say it's a premonition.

You may also feel very drained or low in energy after a psychic premonition, although this could be due to anxiety as well since stressing and agonizing over something can take a mental toll and make you feel exhausted throughout the day and afterward. Hence, this isn't a sure way to tell if it's a premonition, but psychic premonitions do make one feel tired, especially in the case of beginners, as they don't know yet how to use the energy of the universe for help.

Using just your own reserve of energy is usually not the best way to go about psychic practice, as it is limited (as opposed to that of the universe which is unlimited) and can/will be depleted very quickly. If you get a premonition out of nowhere (i.e., receiving a premonition even though you weren't attempting to receive one), it won't leave you a choice to be aided by the universe's energy – but if you are setting out to do a psychic reading, it is important not to use your own limited energy supply and attempt the reading and to receive premonitions unaided.

As you begin awakening your psychic powers, you will begin to notice some changes in your life. This is a sure sign that you're on the right track and that your abilities are growing. Keep an eye out for anything you notice about yourself that's out of the ordinary or if people say you seem different. This is likely because you are vibrating at higher energy now that you've begun to awaken your intuition!

Vivid dreams are one certain sign of this. You will probably notice that the more in tune you are with yourself and your abilities, the more vivid your dreams will be. If you are someone who rarely dreams at all, or rarely remembers your dreams (and if you do it's just vague images and feelings), you will notice an increase in your dreams, and you can recall them more vividly. This is because once your psychic powers have been awakened, your subconscious is more freed up and less blocked, so dreams flow more naturally. Being more in tune with your intuition also heightens your energy, consciousness, and connection to the spirit world, which can present itself to you in your dreams now that your mind has been more awakened.

Along with vivid dreams and tingling sensations, you may also experience a higher frequency in headaches. If you do, please consult a doctor just to be safe. It could be a sign of your mental capacities straining themselves and becoming tired from the psychic practicing you have been doing. The amount of energy you have to use to connect with and focus on your intuition and the psychic realm is great, and even if you tap into the energy of the universe, it can still be a great strain and a burden for a beginner psychic's brain to bear. However, fear not – the headaches should begin to dissipate as you progress and develop your abilities and become stronger and more focused. Eventually, as you become more experienced and in touch with your intuition, psychic readings can become like second nature – and while they are likely still to be tiring, the headaches should subside unless you are doing a particularly difficult reading or a reading requiring a substantial amount of energy, focus, and time. If they do not cease, again, please talk to your doctor about your symptoms. This is important to remember for all symptoms, aches, and pains that can be associated with psychic reading, etc. It's always better to be safe and get them checked, as psychic ability is only one possible explanation.

You may also notice that your other senses become heightened now that you are on the path to psychic awareness. If you've noticed that you no longer need the subtitles turned on when you're watching a movie, your pallet has changed slightly, your eyes seem sharper than usual, or colors become more vivid, you're more sensitive to certain fabrics, and you can pick up and pinpoint scents with much more ease, this can be attributed to your increased psychic potential. After all, you're heightening your sixth sense; it's only natural that the others increase in ability as well. Now, if you get frustrated because you still need your glasses even though your psychic abilities are increasing, just remember that becoming a psychic isn't a cure to anything. It's not going to suddenly allow you to see with 20/20 vision or give you a refined pallet; it may simply elevate your senses slightly, that's all. It's just a sign of increased power.

The more your psychic powers start to show themselves, the higher your vibration becomes. The higher your vibration and energy become, the less time you will want to spend around negative people or doing negative things. Don't be surprised if, while on your psychic journey, your eyes are opened to the negativity and negative habits of some of the people in your life. This is a completely normal part of the psychic journey, and you may end up feeling the need to remove certain people from your life or cease doing certain negative activities that you used to partake in. Unnecessary drama, rudeness, gossip, harmful behavior, etc., are all examples of things which you will begin to have the strong urge to avoid or cease. This is not to say you can't indulge in your favorite reality TV show from time to time, or cut a friend out of your life because they are struggling with an addiction or because they are having a rough day and get angry at you or are negative in the sense that they are sad and maybe struggle with depression. However, people who are always constantly negative and want to drag others down with them are no one you want to be around. If it feels right for you and like it will ultimately bring you happiness and empower you on your journey, then it's best that you remove these people (as gently as possible, without being rude or mean about it, be polite and sensitive if you believe they are owed that) or stop doing these things which bring negativity into your life. Negativity is extremely draining to non-psychics so you can imagine what it does to someone who is likely going to be quite vulnerable to the emotions, thoughts, and energy of others. This is why it is best for psychics to avoid negativity.

An increase or development of psychometry is also common for new psychics. Psychometry is when you can sense the energy or history related to an object just by touching it. Eventually, you may even have premonitions associated with the object, but while you're still a beginner, you may just notice that you can sense the energy of a certain object, often not on purpose. This is quite common in antique stores. Brushing against an old silver mirror, locket, item of jewelry, or any sort of old heirloom may bring you an odd sense of longing seemingly for no reason, but this may be due to the history of the item or the item's owner. Perhaps the item was given to them by the love of their life who then died or left them or who maybe they were forbidden to see. This would explain the feeling of longing associated with the object. It usually occurs with older objects or objects which have been through a lot, and whose current or previous owners have been through a lot. It can be articles of clothing, jewelry, art, furniture – even when entering a house many psychics can feel the energy related to it and its history/old owners. If you are moving out soon and go to look at an open house, to get a sense of whether the house is right for you, also take into account the energy of the place. Run your hands over the walls, counters, and furniture in every room. This should give you a good indication of whether there is an excess of negative energy or not, or whether you/whomever you're moving with and the house will be a good energetic fit. You'll often hear of people's hair standing on end and having a sense of evil or negative energy when entering a house, and then later finding out a murder or some other horrific event took place there at some point. This is because they are picking up the energy of the space through psychometry. People with more developed intuition and psychic abilities are more prone to picking up energy, so if you begin sensing things like this when you touch them, it's a good sign that you're on the right track.

Four Types of Psychic Intuition

Now that we're discussing what your psychic intuition feels like and some signs that your powers are developing, let's take a look at the different types of psychic intuition and define them:

- Clairaudience
- Clairvoyance
- Clairsentience
- Clair cognizance

You may not have heard these terms before, so here is a brief description of each.

Clairaudience

 is when it sounds like someone is speaking directly in your mind. Not in the same way as people with certain mental illnesses – this is more of a short answer to a question, or advice, and it shouldn't sound/feel harsh or discordant. The word "clair" means clear, and "audience" is from "audire" meaning to hear, so you are psychically "hearing" these messages, though usually, it is within the mind. It can sound similar to when you act out a conversation in your head, or similar to how you hear people talking in dreams.

These sounds and messages can come from your spirit guides or from the spirit of someone in your life who has died.

Clairvoyance

is when you see images in your mind's eye that hold psychic significance. "Voyance" meaning vision, so clear vision. The next time an image springs into your mind, seemingly out of the blue, try to analyze it. It may have a symbolic (or very literal) meaning about something coming up in your life, or it may explain something you've been thinking or worrying about. Clairvoyance won't be a very specific flash into the future where you can see exactly an event that will happen as a movie in your mind – like how they show it on TV shows. It will be a subtle image or "vision" in your mind's eye. You may have had clairvoyant messages in the past without realizing it! Some examples of what is classified as a clairvoyant message could be colors, numbers or letters, words, pictures or images of people, objects, animals, places, or anything symbolic.

Clairsentience

(clear feeling) is probably the most common of the four. It is when you feel something is going to happen. If you've ever heard someone use the phrase "I can just feel it" or "this doesn't feel right" this is clairsentience. Clairsentience is often called your "gut feeling" or your instinct. Another aspect of clairsentience is being able to sense the emotions of others. Maybe you feel a wave of sadness before your friend walks into a room, and then they tell you their mother has passed away. Maybe you're on the phone with your friend who has a broken right leg, and you feel a brief pain in your right leg, even before knowing they broke it. Maybe you see your pet and suddenly burst into tears overwhelmed by sadness for no apparent reason, and within a week, your pet dies. These are examples of clairsentience.

Claircognizance

(clear knowing) is when your intuition helps you figure something out that your rational brain can't, something you're maybe stuck on. For example, if you're stuck in traffic, should you risk taking the upcoming exit to get out of it and take the backroad, or will that end up taking longer? You inexplicably decide to wait it out and soon traffic has cleared, and you're on your way. This is claircognizance. If you've ever heard someone say, "I just know" and they have no evidence to prove their certainty or no way of knowing but end up being right – that is claircognizance.

So how do you tell whether you're just having an ordinary thought or whether it's a psychic message? The messages and premonitions can often be quite subtle, but the way to tell is if something (image, sound, feeling, certainty) just pops into your mind with absolutely no relation to what you were just thinking about. This is probably a psychic message and not a thought. Usually, these psychic messages are quite strong as well, not a little afterthought at the back of your mind. However, sometimes they are quieter communications, so with anything that comes into your mind seemingly unprovoked, it's always best to try and look at it closer and analyze it – it may have some psychic significance.

With these four channels of psychic communication, if you just take a deeper look at the next sound, image, feeling or thought that springs into your mind unbidden, you may find some relevant psychic meaning to it. The message(s) will help you gain information, receive communications from the spirit realm (spirit guides, passed on loved ones, etc.), or reveal premonitions or predictions to you, that your other five senses can't. You may already have read this list and honed in on one of the four that you feel more connected with or that you think one of them will definitely come more naturally than the others. Maybe you have used one or more of these in the past, whether you realized it at the time or not. Maybe you've already noticed that you have more of an ability for one than the others. That is likely the one you will be strongest at and the channel you will receive the clearest most powerful messages in, at least for now. I don't mean you can't practice with the other types and strengthening them. There are many psychics who, for example, started off naturally talented at clairvoyance and receiving clairvoyant messages, but as they practiced, they gradually became more powerful at, and mastered, clairsentience and that became their strongest intuitive channel. This is just one example, but it's to show that you're never stuck in just one situation or skillset with just one option!

Although if you wish to keep the one you have a knack for as your strongest ability, then by all means. Remember, psychic ability is like a muscle!

Each psychic has a specific way in which their power and intuition manifests itself, and it's often related to who they are and what sort of person they are. Everyone, regardless of ability, has one of four psychic personalities. You are either a spiritual intuitive, a physical intuitive, an emotional intuitive, or a mental intuitive. So how do you find out which kind you are and fits your psychic abilities? Well, each one manifests itself differently, and there are certain traits associated with each type that you can look over to aid you in discovering which one you resonate with the most, and which one seems to be more you. There is no official test, but each psychic personality is defined in the following paragraphs – and hopefully, you can get a sense of which one fits for you.

Physical intuitive are the ones that have deep attachments to important objects, and usually, psychometry (sensing things via touching physical objects) comes naturally to them. They are the ones who are more likely to use objects like tarot cards, crystal balls, palm reading or tasseography (tea leaf reading) to determine things about a person or the future and perform psychic readings. They are very literally hands-on when it comes to sensing energy, relying on physical presence or moving their hands close to an object or person to get a sense of things. This makes them the ones most likely to be drawn to the art of psychic healing, or the ones that usually have a natural talent for the practice. They are often homebodies and love organizing their home, furniture, and decorations according to their interests. Their home isn't simply some space for them to eat and go to sleep at night – it is their temple and haven from the outside world, and it showcases a piece of who they are. They spend a solid amount of time at home and often have a lot of clutter and trinkets around the house. They also thoroughly enjoy spending time in nature and grounding themselves.

Mental intuitives are the analysts. They will think things over repeatedly, turning it over and over in their minds until they find an explanation for something until they yield a result. They always make sure they take into account every little detail, checking and double checking. They don't ever want to miss anything, and they're not big risk takers, nor are they very spontaneous. Mental Intuitives are more likely to be clairvoyant or clairaudient and receive psychic messages via imagery or sound in their mind, as this is where they spend most of their time. They tend to "live in their head" so to speak and can go for hours on end with merely the company of their own thoughts, just thinking. They are going to need the most information and ask for the most detail when they sit down to do a reading for someone. They are the ones to logic their way through something – logic, reason, and rationality are what they live by. When working on something, whether it be a psychic related task or otherwise, they generally have a good ability to focus and stay focused on what they are doing. They also tend to have somewhat academic interests, although this isn't always the case.

The Art of Crystal Gazing Or Scrying

Crystal gazing, or scrying as it used to be called, is another natural human ability that is easy to learn once you have gone through the basic psychic training given in Psychic **Development Level 1**. Most people scry quite naturally, never even realizing what they are doing.

Also, as hypnotists who use a focus for their work well know, as you stare into a crystal and enter into an alpha or meditative state, there is a tendency for many people to fall even deeper, entering a trance state.

So, how do people use scrying in their everyday lives without even realizing it? Let me draw your attention to many ways you are using it yourself already. Do you remember lying on your back looking up at the clouds and then suddenly seeing a woman's face in one of them, or an animal in another? That is a beginning form of scrying. And remember waking up in the morning, and while your mind is lingering in that consciousness midway between waking and sleeping and you don't quite know you are really awake yet, you see a face peering at you from the folds of the sheets? As you become aware of what you are looking at you quickly try to focus on it, and as your mind enters a normal waking state and your focus changes, the face disappears. This is another example of beginner level scrying, and everyone does it! It happens readily when you are in that not-quite-awake stage, which is the equivalent of the alpha state we require to do most of our psychic divination work!

So, you know already that you have the ability to scry. You merely have to learn to do it consciously, and to focus your thoughts in the direction of seeing a particular thing as opposed to random objects and things.

I recall teaching a class on crystal gazing back in the 1980's in which I forgot, myself, to focus on anything specific. I saw an American army jeep traveling across the desert with a pyramid in the background and the Islamic moon and star configuration overhead. I didn't think much of it at the time, since I had asked no question and had no specific focus... until many years later, in Desert Storm and after, there were many American army jeeps there. I was being shown a political future that I failed to understand because I had no focus.

In scrying or crystal gazing it often is difficult to interpret what we see. To make this somewhat easier, I always enter my scrying meditation with a question, or a focus in mind, which I write down. I also date my page, since like many other forms of divination, my scrying may give me a look into the future. In fact, it is the nature of this form of divination to see into the future. Most of the things you see will relate to future events once you learn to scry. Nostradamus is the most famous seer in history. He used an aventurine crystal ball, combined with astrology, to scry events that would not transpire for hundreds of years. But because his focus was not specific, it is unlikely that he even understood his predictions himself at the time he wrote them down. Interpreting these images that he copiously recorded is still the work of untold numbers of scholars today.

For me, writing my focus down is imperative to both keeping my vision on target, and also to being able to interpret the things I see, so they may be of use to me and the people around me now.

Sometimes the things you see in your crystal gazing or scrying are factual. The previous image of an American army jeep in the desert is an example. This was an actual, factual representation of something to come in the future. But often the images you see are more like dream images... they are symbolic as opposed to factual. For example, I may see an image of a young man with stars floating around him. How should I interpret that, unless I have posed a question? That image could mean the young man will be a star, is moving to Texas (the star is the state symbol of Texas), is getting a promotion, or will be arrested by several sheriffs. If I have asked no question, I really can't interpret this symbol at all. I can merely write it down, and wait for something to transpire that fits. If I haven't asked a question, it is possible I won't even recognize the young man. It could be a random scenario that takes place in a future not my own. But if I have posed a question, I can interpret the image relative to the question, using my experience with dream interpretation as a guide.

This is one of the reasons I have encouraged you to spend so much time on dream interpretation throughout your psychic development studies. Your dreams are a symbolic form of communication between you and your Higher Self and guides, and the better you get at interpreting them the better you will be at interpreting the psychic information received in your readings!

Types of Scrying Tools

After my description of beginning-level scrying automatically occurring when you shape clouds or do other similar activities, you will appreciate it when I tell you that you can scry in almost anything.

There used to be an old woman on Long Island everyone called the 'egg lady.' She used to take the white of an egg, put it into a clear bowl or cup with some water, give it a stir with a fork to create some ripples and depth, and scry out your future in one of the most accurate readings I've ever seen. She was wonderful at interpreting what she saw… but her use of the white of an egg in clear water was a stroke of genius. Try it when we learn the technique for crystal gazing or scrying later in the chapter. It really is very effective.

Water lends itself to scrying. As a matter of fact, water-scrying or water-divination is probably one of the easiest techniques to master. This form of divination is called a Lunar form (your scrying will actually be better the closer it gets to a full or new moon) and of course the moon is associated with water. I have successfully scryed in a bowl of clear water, a bowl of water with a drop of oil and a drop of vinegar swirled into it, a bowl of water with a drop of ink and a drop of oil swirled in it, water with a drop of food coloring and vinegar in it, in the bubbles of a hot tub, in a tidal pool at the beach, in a mud puddle, and in my morning coffee. I invite you to experiment with all of these once you learn the proper technique. Of course, you should never forget your protection either, unless the images you scry are totally spontaneous, which does happen sometimes. When it does, as soon as you become aware you've just received an image, write it down and date it. If you continue to scry, do your protections before you start to do it again.

So, obviously you don't have to be rich and be able to afford a real crystal ball to be able to scry. Any old puddle will do! However, many of you reading this ARE interested in purchasing or making a special scrying tool. Let me discuss some of them here with you.

Scrying mirror – These are simple thing to make. Take any concave clear glass dish and paint the outside surface flat black. You can make wormwood tea and rub the surface with the herb tea to enhance it as a scrying tool. Wormwood is an herb that enhances scrying. Or, you can purchase a fancy scrying mirror and rub it with wormwood tea. The scrying mirror you make will actually be easier to work with, because in making it you added your own vibration to it. Glass itself is an insulator, so you will find by and large that glass balls, bowls or mirrors are difficult to work with initially, until you build up enough of an energy field around them, through use, that you can readily scry in them. An experienced practitioner can easily scry in just about any surface, but a beginner does best with either a tool he or she has made, or something made of natural materials, like crystal.

Real mirror – This is not my favorite tool because it requires that you learn to focus past your own face, which many people find difficult to do. However, once the technique is mastered it is not a bad tool. Remember, though that a mirror is glass.

Acrylic crystal ball – I want to warn you against this. My own earliest crystal ball was an acrylic ball that I thought was great because it was shaped with a flat bottom, and it was huge. The first time I tried to use it I sat staring into it for three hours (not recommended) and came away with nothing more than a headache. It took many, many hours and years of use by my students in classes before that ball developed a strong enough energy field that it could lend help to the scryer.

Crystal balls – These are the most exciting. Crystal balls are made of rock crystal. These may be clear quartz, rose quartz, amethyst, or smoky quartz, all of which are mostly transparent, or of black onyx, aventurine, hematite, or other opaque stone – most people find the transparent stones easier to work with, especially ones with lots of faults and occlusions that catch the eye's fantasy. The very expensive perfectly clear quartz sphere shown in all the movies is really not as good a scrying tool as the less perfect sphere or egg or even slab of crystal that is full of cracks, bubbles, ridges, and other imperfections that catch your eye and are readily transfigured into scenes and movement as you conduct your scrying session. The real beauty of working with crystals though is that they bring their own energy to the session.

Crystal gazing, or scrying, takes enormous amounts of your energy, especially for the beginner... it helps to work with a tool that can supply some of the energy. In time, as you learn to do this you won't have to work so hard at it, and it will take much less energy to do. Until then though, it is important to keep your time that you are gazing limited, and to work with a tool that either aids your energy level, such as a crystal, or that at least does not take energy itself to use (like an acrylic ball or a glass ball).

Selecting A Crystal or Scrying Tool

A scrying implement or crystal ball is a very personal divination tool. It is NOT something that someone else should pick out for you. You should first investigate the various types of tools I've discussed, and see which ones appeal to you. Once you have narrowed it down, if the tools you are interested in are to be purchased, you should begin to shop for the exact one you want. Not all such tools are created equal, even if they look the same! The scrying tool you ultimately pick should be something that resonates to YOU... that you feel innately comfortable with. In essence, it should be the one that jumps off the shelf and says, "I'm it!"

I remember clearly when I first found and purchased my own crystal ball, a rather small (about 2.5 inches by 1.5 inches) smoky quartz crystal 'egg.' (Yes, you are getting the idea… when it comes to crystals size does not matter, provided the surface you are looking in is large enough for you to see an image.)

I had walked into a makeshift store that had been set up outside a seminar I was attending. From the doorway of the store I looked about 25 feet across the store to a glass display case holding crystals, and saw, from that distance, a miniature stagecoach complete with a team of four horses racing across the face of the crystal. I knew immediately it was meant to be mine, and purchased it, not even questioning a rather hefty price. I have never been sorry.

Most people don't have quite that obvious an introduction to their crystal or scrying tools. For most, it is a sense of attraction, and when you hold it, (which you should do for a while to let your own vibration merge with its) it feels right.

Charging and Caring for a Crystal or Scrying Tool

Is there anything special I should do to charge or care for my crystal or scrying tool? Yes, there is. First of all, once you have chosen your own scrying implement it will gradually become an extension of yourself, as you use it. You should not let other people touch it. Would you let someone touch intimate parts of yourself without permission? I thought not. Someone touching or using your crystal or scrying tool is really the same thing, as you will one day see.

Secondly, your scrying tool will probably need to be grounded and cleared when you first get it. Remember, many other people, from its manufacture to its sale, have undoubtedly touched it, maybe even tried it out. You will need to clear that vibration from it.

There are several ways you might go about grounding or clearing it. (Incidentally, you might also apply these to your pendulum if it should ever feel dirty to you, or if you should have trouble obtaining accurate information with it at some point.) The easiest way is to let it rest under running water for 10 or 15 minutes. In most cases this is adequate to clear a new crystal. Or, you might soak it in water with three pinches of sea salt for that same time period, or if it feels very dirty, overnight. Or try burying it or letting it rest beneath a pine, oak, or ash tree overnight. These are particularly good trees for this, since all aid the expansion of the Third Eye outward as in scrying. All will also energize your scrying tool as they ground it.

Crystal gazing or scrying is a lunar psychic ability. Your scrying implement likes the night, likes the dark, likes the moon. You should charge it by holding it in your right hand as you meditate, at night, on a full moon. When you are finished, leave it on a windowsill in the light of the full moon to finish charging. Remove it from the windowsill before sunlight. It does not like the light of the sun. It will lose its lunar charge if left in sunlight and you will have to start over again!

Your scrying implement or crystal should not be exposed to the light of day except when you are actually using it. So, you should wrap it in a soft dark natural fiber cloth like silk or cotton. Then, store it in a dark place, like a drawer or a box.

When you do your actual crystal gazing with it, you will find that you get best results in dim lighting conditions, such as in a room lit only by a candle or a dim light... you must have some light to see by, but inevitably the light will reflect in the crystal and becomes a distraction... you will need to learn to let the light that is reflected become merely one more imperfection in the ball or other tool that you are using, and that you blend into the image you will see.

You may also rub ANY scrying tool with a tea of wormwood herb or yarrow to enhance its ability to help you to scry. (Yes, that is correct. The proper tool will be a help to your scrying, not a hindrance!)

On Crystal Gazing or Scrying

Unfortunately, most of the books that I have read on crystal gazing or scrying over the years did more to confuse my natural ability to scry then they did to aid it. Most talk about the ball or scrying implement clouding over, and/or becoming hazy around the edges, and then eventually the clouds and haze disappear and you see wonderful clear images, usually around the edges of the scrying tool. This is confusing at best, and even misleading.

What clouds over is not the ball, it is your vision, as your mind shifts focus to the alpha wave level required for scrying. When you see a haze around the edges of your ball or scrying implement, it is not really that you are seeing a haze, it is that you are using the soft-focus gaze learned in Psychic Development Level 2 to see auras, which utilizes the rods, as opposed to the cones of your eyes, and produces this hazy effect around the edges.

As a reminder, you attain the alpha level by first meditating to still your mind, which is a part of our protection and invocation of guides, and you use the soft focus vision by looking obliquely, that is, indirectly, at the crystal or scrying tool – this has the effect of first clouding the edges of the crystal, then making things there appear to attain greater clarity. It forces you to look with your eyes' rod cells, the black and white receptors, as opposed to the cones, the color receptors. Any color you see in your scrying tool (and you will see color) is strictly seen clairvoyantly. Your eyes will not really see it.

And when you first see images appear out of all this, it will actually be the imperfections of the ball or implement reorganizing themselves into an image that your creative imagination is giving you. This becomes a jump off point to actually start to see images and symbols in your tool.

Now, follow the next exercise to do your first real scrying!

Exercise #1: A Technique for Crystal Gazing or Scrying

1. Darken the room and leave on only a single dim light source. Have paper and pen ready. Have your crystal ball or scrying tool set to go. Many people like to place their tool on a black cloth, finding this less distracting than the tabletop they may see through it. Sit comfortably at a table. Set an alarm clock for a 15-minute interval.

2. Be sure to turn off the phone, and be sure animals and children are where they cannot become a distraction.

3. Sit with your spine erect. Take three deep diaphragmatic breaths to ground and center. Close your eyes as you do this, and see any tension or negativity in you swirl down your body and out into the ground beneath you.

4. Place your palms in your lap facing upward, and bring as much energy as you can into yourself through them, and at the same time through your Crown Center and Third Eye Center. Breathe in as you do this, breathing in as much energy as possible. With each exhalation continue to ground.

5. When you feel clear and grounded, put yourself in the white light of protection.

6. Put yourself in your protective energy balloon.

7. Recite your prayer.

8. Ask for their help in your work today. If you receive an impression that is negative, you should not proceed today, or should not ask the intended question.

9. Now, open your eyes, and date your paper and write out your question.

10. You may either pick the crystal or scrying implement up or leave it on the table and peer down into it or sideways at it. Experiment with position and placement until you find what is comfortable.

11. Gaze into the crystal. Don't stare. Your eyes should be in soft-focus. If you need to blink, go ahead. Allow your breathing to become deep and regular, and to relax your eyes still further as you breathe.

12. If your eyes want to wander around the crystal, allow them to.

13. You may or may not perceive a haze over the surface and/or around the sides of the crystal. Ignore it.

14. If you perceive an image off to the side of your gaze, do not move your eyes to look at it, just allow yourself to register the image with your peripheral vision. Continue to gaze with the same soft-focus attention and make a mental note of any other images that appear.

15. During your session, hold your mind to the best of your ability either on your question, or in a still and receptive state. If you allow it to wander, the images that appear in the crystal will either stop or become disjointed, reflecting your mental state.

16. When 15 minutes are up, bring your attention back to the room you are in, exhaling deeply to ground yourself again as you do. Write down whatever you saw, exactly as you saw it, and in sequence. Be sure to write down the seemingly inconsequential things, like a string of lights, or your own reflection that you might have seen. Once interpreted, even these things can have significance!

17. Now before you finish, thank your guides for their help, and release your protective energy balloon.

Take the time now, to interpret what you saw in light of the question you had asked.

Congratulations! You have just completed your first controlled scrying session. In time you can become very adept at this, and it may even become one of your tools of choice for obtaining future information.

You should also note that practice with scrying will be an invaluable aid to developing your clairvoyant skills to where you can begin to see people and symbols around other people, in their energy fields. And eventually, if you decide to study spirit communication (mediumship) it will help you to develop the ability to see the spirits clairvoyantly as well.

Evaluating Psychic Experiences

D o You Recall?
Can you remember your first psychic experience? Some of you can probably recall it clearly, while others may have little or no recognition of any psychic experience at all. Chances are that it came at a very early age. You may be able to find an older family member or acquaintance who can remember that

you talked about some incident that you have consciously forgotten. It could have been a series of circumstances or a single event.

All of those past experiences are stored in your unconscious mind. Even as you read these words, you may call to mind something that you haven't thought about in years. Some of you may have powerful memories connected to "unexplainable experiences" in your past. As you progress through these pages, the goal is for you to be able to define and reconnect with your special psychic gifts.

Here are a few tips for trying to remember your early psychic experiences:

> Allow yourself to be open to recalling psychic memory flashes, and don't overanalyze them.
>
> Don't expect to get all of the memory at once.
>
> Keep notes of your psychic memory flashes so that you can refer back to them.
>
> Once you have an idea of a possible psychic flash, talk to others who might have been aware of it at the time it happened.
>
> Use basic relaxation techniques to help you focus on your early psychic memory.
>
> PRACTICE POINTER

Whenever you are connecting to your third eye, give yourself the suggestion that you may always end your connection by opening your eyes, taking a deep breath, and connecting to your conscious mind.

Count Down

As you count yourself down, you may feel yourself sinking deeper and deeper, feeling more and more relaxed with each count. It is a very pleasant feeling, and you look forward to the next number as you count yourself downward. As you focus on your third eye, you may allow yourself to relax more and more as you open up your psychic memories. You may allow any muscles that you feel are stiff to relax. If you are ready, take a deep breath, exhale, and start counting:

5. Breathe in and out, and feel yourself relaxing more and more with each breath. Let yourself relax your muscles. As you mention the next number to yourself, you may feel yourself connecting more and more strongly with your third eye. You may feel yourself going deeper and deeper into your unconscious mind, opening up to your early psychic memories.

4. Feel yourself going deeper and deeper as you feel the connection to your third eye becoming stronger and stronger. You may breathe in and out, slowly, relaxing more and more with each breath. You may feel yourself

getting closer and closer to your memories of your early psychic experiences.

3. As you breathe slowly, you may feel yourself relaxing more and more. You may feel yourself going deeper and deeper into your unconscious mind. As you get closer and closer to zero, you will be more and more connected with your unconscious mind. You will be ready to come in contact with your early childhood psychic memories.

2. You are getting closer and closer, as you sink deeper and deeper. You are relaxing more and more, and your psychic memories will be ready for you to access when you get to zero. As you breathe in and out slowly, you will allow yourself to relax more and more. You can feel your connection to your third eye more and more.

1. You are almost there. You may feel very comfortable, relaxed, and safe. You know you may always come back to a conscious state any time you want by opening your eyes, taking a deep breath, exhaling, and feeling relaxed and positive. You may allow yourself to go deeper and deeper as you count slowly backward from five to zero, each number ten times stronger than the last.

0. You may feel the connection to your third eye even more strongly than before as you are now ready to access the unconscious memories of your early childhood experiences. Anything you see, feel, hear, taste, or smell

will help you to remember your early childhood psychic experiences.

PRACTICE POINTER

While you are in a relaxed and comfortable state, you may let your unconscious memory recall images from the past that are about your early psychic experiences at a pace that is good and comfortable for you. Be aware that you can open your eyes and come back to full consciousness any time you want, feeling relaxed, calm, and refreshed.

Count Back Up

When you are ready, you may count slowly back up to your conscious mind. When you reach five, you will remember any images you may have recalled relating to early psychic experiences.

1. You are coming up and slowly releasing your connection to the third eye as you count toward five.

2. Breathe slowly and comfortably, as you count yourself back up.

3. You are getting closer and closer to the surface of your conscious mind.

4. Slowly release your connection to the third eye.

5. Now you may come fully back to the surface of your conscious mind as you release your connection to the third

eye. Take a deep breath, open your eyes, and exhale. You may feel relaxed and positive about your connection to any early childhood psychic memories that you may have recalled.

Each time you perform this exercise, you may have different results. Don't expect a specific outcome. Each time you try, you may find more and different memories coming up to the surface of your conscious mind. Once you open the communication channel and continue to connect to it, the flow will become easier to access.

Near-Death Experiences and Lessons

Have you ever had a near-death experience? Was there ever a close call, during which you were inches or moments away from potential death? Did you survive a bad fall or a blow to the head? Did you have other traumatic experiences when you were young in which your mind was an important key to your survival?

Near-death experiences come in many different ways, but going through such an experience may have "jump-started" your third eye into being more open to psychic intuition.

When you go through a traumatic experience, all of your senses experience a surge in the intensity of the power of their perception. In some cases, your view of the world changes dramatically. You know something's different, but you're not sure what it is.

Children and Near-Death Experiences

A near-death experience in early childhood may often go unnoticed. Kids get into all kinds of trouble. They fall from trees, get trapped underwater, trip down the stairs, survive a car accident, or tumble off the playground swings. In some cases, such a close call may grow out of an unconscious need to escape a traumatic situation such as abuse or an emotionally unstable family.

A PSYCHIC TRUTH

Edgar Cayce had several early-life experiences that could have contributed to his psychic development. His skull was pierced with a nail at age three; he watched his grandfather die from a horseback accident; and at age fifteen he was hit in the spine with a ball. This later experience seemed to help connect him to his psychic healing knowledge.

Can you think of events in your life that may have affected your psychic ability? You are the sum total of your life to this very moment. Each new, passing moment will bring about change. As you learn to become in tune with your life, you will be more aware of your psychic abilities.

As a Child . . .

The dreams you had in your childhood could very well have been psychic in nature. Dreams, like other psychic experiences, may deal with past events or future events, or they may provide insight into situations that are occurring at the time of the dream. Dreams are a great way to receive psychic information because the conscious analytical mind is at rest, and you are open to communication from your unconscious and your Universal Mind.

Think about the dreams you had as a child. Do you remember any? If so, can you recall if they had a theme? Did you have a certain dream that occurred over and over? Can you identify the historical time period and/or location of any dreams?

Did you have symbolic dreams that may not have made sense when you had them, but that you might better understand at this point in your life? Did you have any dreams that identified situations in your life before you experienced them? Did you have recurring nightmares? Did you have dreams that were different but followed a related theme?

Did you have dreams in which dead relatives or others who had passed over communicated with you? Did you have angels, guides, or other beings or animals come to you in your sleep to comfort you and/or offer you advice? Did you ever have dreams of flying or going to places that you had never been before? Do you recall any other types of dreams that may have been of a psychic nature when you were a child?

A PSYCHIC TRUTH

Here is an example of a second-sight experience. Mary remembers that as a girl, she played in the woods with other children. They taught her how to play their games. It was only later that she learned their games and clothing were from the Revolutionary War period.

You can investigate the answers to these questions in a relaxed state, as you contact your third eye. Trust your intuitive mind to give you the right answers. If you cannot remember anything, it's possible that you did not use dreams as a part of your early psychic development.

Second Sight

When you were a child, did you ever see things that were invisible to others? Did you have "imaginary friends" to play with? Could you find your way to or around a place where you had never been before?

What other experiences that might not be explainable to others did you have as a child? Did you ever have a visit from fairies or guides? Do you recall any contacts that could be considered otherworldly, such as with beings from another planet?

Déjà Vu and Learning from Past Lives

Did you ever, as a child, go to a strange place and know you had been there before? Did you experience something and feel that it had already happened? Childhood déjà vu is a phenomenon that can happen naturally. As a child, your view of reality is different be- cause your early psychic experiences aren't limited by the boundaries that society has set for adults.

Sometimes déjà vu is so strong that second sight engages, and the experience becomes so real that the person having the experience loses touch with reality. This happens to a child more easily than to an adult, but such experiences often stay with a child into adulthood.

Past Lives

During childhood, we may still have memories from our past lives; these memories are gradually forgotten as we grow older. Do you recall any early childhood memories that can give you clues about your past lives? Did you know things about family members from different lifetimes? Did you ever act as if your role in the family were different than it should have been? Did you ever tell your family stories about other lifetimes?

Chances are, some of your psychic intuitions have come from what you've retained from your past. The more of these soul memories you can recall, the more you will find a connection to your psychic gifts.

Guidance from Within

Your inner guidance system is your connection to the Universal Mind as well as the sum total of all the wisdom and experiences you've accumulated up to this point in time. Remember that your inner wisdom and experiences come from your soul and that they transcend this one lifetime. The purpose of your inner guidance system is to help you stay on course with your life map.

Think of your guidance system as your conscience. It lets you know when something you may have said or done or left undone is inappropriate. Of course, you have the power to override your inner guidance system, and chances are you do it all the time. Everyone does. Have you ever caught yourself saying, "Why didn't I listen to myself?" It is only natural to get caught in the battle between your ego and your conscience. One is authoritative and looking for instant satisfaction, while the other wants to do the right thing.

Building Trust and Confidence

It takes time to build trust and confidence in your inner guidance system. It is the same as developing any other skill. It takes patience and the willingness to risk making mistakes as you work toward your goals. Many people are overwhelmed easily and give up because the end goal seems unobtainable.

The key to developing your trust and confidence is to start with one step at a time. If you only focus on an obstacle that is too big to climb, you will never have the opportunity to get to the top. If you work toward a small and easily achievable goal, when you reach it, you will have accomplished your short-range objective.

You will then have more confidence that you can make it to your next goal. And before you know it, you have accomplished your long-term goal.

These small reachable goals are usually in tune with your inner guidance system. Each step of the way provides a balance. Giving yourself permission to take a small risk, and knowing that you have a safety net created by past success, you will become better and better at reaching toward the unknown. There is a great thrill of adventure when you are traveling in sync with your life map, in tune with your inner guidance system.

A PSYCHIC TRUTH

Your own answer may come from within yourself in the form of a dream, or it may just "pop out" of your unconscious mind. It could come when you are offering advice to others, and yet the message may be for yourself. It could appear as a recurring thought that you just can't get out of your mind until you address it.

Tune In and Develop Your Gift

To tune in to your inner guidance system, you need to practice. The more you focus on developing your intuitive gifts, the more they will respond to you. If you can find a regular time once a day when you can focus on communicating with your unconscious and your Universal Mind, you will develop a habit of connecting to your inner guidance system. You will add a posthypnotic suggestion to help you with this automatic process.

If you would like to try this exercise, find a comfortable place, either sitting or lying down, loosen your clothes, take a deep breath of air, and slowly exhale. You may now focus on your third eye. As you slowly breathe in and out, you may be aware that you have many muscles; some of them are tight, and some of them are relaxed.

The more you allow the tight muscles to relax, the more relaxed you will become. In a few moments you may count down from five to zero, feeling yourself going deeper and deeper with each number. As you go deeper and deeper, you will feel your connection to your third eye becoming stronger and stronger.

Feel the Connection

As you feel the connection getting stronger, you will be aware that you are receiving a beam of light and energy that is flowing into your third eye from the Universe. This beam is good and positive, and it flows freely into your inner guidance system, carrying the wisdom of your soul.

If you are ready, you may start with the first number:

5. You are going deeper and deeper into the Universal Flow. Breathe slowly in and out as you feel the connection through your third eye getting stronger and stronger.

4. You are feeling the Universal Flow as it is received by your inner guidance system. You feel more and more relaxed with each count.

3. You may feel the vibrations of the Universe. As you go to the next number, you are more and more in tune with the flow.

2. You are getting closer and closer. Your breathing relaxes more and more. You are going deeper and deeper.

1. You are almost at the point of a deep and powerful connection to the Universal Mind. You look forward to the last number as you take another breath and go deeper and deeper.

0. You are one with your Universal Mind and your inner guidance system.

Once the connection is complete, take a few moments to enjoy the strength and peace of the Universe. You may think of many thoughts or concentrate on just one. If you need help or guidance or have a worry, ask the Universal Mind to provide assistance and affirmation that you are in tune with your life map.

Synchronize Internal and External Messages

In addition to your channel of internal communication, you have an external guidance system of old souls who have completed their life journeys and wait to assist you. As Edgar Cayce said, the external guidance system is an "invisible empire" that exists around you.

Your external guidance system comes from the outside. It is a form of external communication from another person or entity. For instance, you may see auras or energies around others that allow you to receive helpful information. Or you may get a warning from a particular person or even from a geographic location.

Remember, these communications from the Universe can materialize at any time in almost any form imaginable, from a cloud in the sky to an encounter with an animal. All you need to do is pay attention.

Experiences of Synchronicity

One kind of external guidance experience is synchronicity. Have you ever found yourself in the right place at the right time? For some reason, exactly when you most need it, the phone rings with an answer to a dilemma. Perhaps it's an unexpected amount of money that you receive just in time to hold off a financial disaster. It could come in the mail, from a lottery ticket, from a long-forgotten debt someone owes you, or as a gift.

It is very easy to overlook synchronicity. It happens so naturally that it may not even be noticed. It's like watching a magician intently so that you may learn the trick. The magic happens right under your nose while you are focused on something else.

You're Not Alone

Are forces like synchronicity and the other external forms that your messages take all just coincidence, luck, or fate? Or is there something else involved? Perhaps you already know that someone is watching out for you. Or maybe you don't believe that there is anything at all.

Do you think that there is a being or a force that the Universe centers upon? Is there a divine purpose or a higher ideal for mankind to get in touch with? Is there a general plan for the cosmos?

A PSYCHIC TRUTH

It's all right to believe your own way. After all, that belief is already inside you. It is okay for you to compare anything you read in this book to your own feelings. The important thing is that it feels right for you.

If you have something or someone looking out for you, do you know who or what it is? You may know exactly, or you may have no idea. Just the possibility that there is something creates the opportunity for hope. You may be comfortable in a specific religion and have conversations with the Divinity to whom you turn for guidance. You may go to the seashore or the mountains and communicate with nature.

Other people believe in guardian angels who are said to watch over us. You may connect these angels to someone in your family or a friend who has passed on to the Other Side. They may come to you in your dreams, or you may feel their presence, especially in times of need.

Whatever you believe in, the purpose of this book is to give you an opportunity to explore your belief and develop your ability to connect to it.

A Short History Of Psychic & Paranormal Abilities

Specific psychic and paranormal abilities go in and out of vogue from one era to another. For much of history various forms of divination were the predominant psychic power called upon or known by the average person. It is only in modern times with the preponderance of movies, books and television shows that other paranormal gifts have received widespread recognition.

Today's entertainment media are good indicators of the paranormal gifts that are currently the most popular with the general public. Recent shows such as Charmed (1998-2006) had main characters with powers of telekinesis, astral projection, divination, scrying, apportation, levitation, past vision, energy healing, teleportation and auric energy power. Multiple shows during the last 15 years have highlighted psychometry where the psychic receives flashes of past events by touching an object that was involved in the event.

Late 1800's to Early 1900's: Going back a few generations to the first decades of the late 1800's and early 1900's, spiritualism and afterlife communication were very popular, as were spiritualist churches where contacting the spirits of the deceased through a medium was the central part of the service.

Middle Ages: In the Middle Ages there was a fascination with fire. Even peasants paid attention to the movement of the flame from an oil lamp or torch (lampadomancy) and looked for signs and portends of the future in the smoke rising from cooking fires and the crackle of pockets of pitch as logs burned (libanomancy).

Wizards of the early Middle Ages would often cast salt onto the floor and interpret the patterns, or use a mixture of various types of mineral salts cast into a fire and interpret the colors (halomancy). Casting pebbles or small rocks into a still pool or running stream and noting the pattern of the ensuing ripples (hydromancy) was another popular technique of the professional diviners. A more advanced form of libanomancy, predicting the future based upon the reaction of incense cast upon hot coals, was also a popular form of divination with the professionals.

Talisman or Lucky Charms have probably been popular since the dawn of time, but became particularly popular during the early Middle Ages when it was not uncommon to purchase an enchanted Talisman from traveling wizards.

Another common form of divination during the Middle Ages that has fallen out of favor in modern times is Mirror Gazing and related methods using reflective surfaces, collectively known as catoptromancy. The psychic Nostradamus, from the 1500's, still heralded today for predictions of many of the world's great events he made that many people feel came true, was said to favor the use of a bowl of ink to exhibit a reflective surface from which he could divine his prophecies.

The paranormal power imbued in a mirror has been a central theme in a couple of key modern and early modern stories, including 'Snow White', where the wicked witch sought an answer by asking, "Mirror, mirror on the wall, who is the fairest of them all?" It was also through the paranormal qualities of a 'Looking Glass', known today as a mirror, that Alice journeyed to Wonderland in Lewis Caroll's fanciful story.

Roman Period: From Julius Caesar to King Philip of Macedonia, history remembers the leaders and the history changing actions they took. But forgotten in the annuls of history are the psychics they consulted before they took the actions. It was common throughout both the Greek and Roman periods for kings, generals and landowners to consult esteemed psychics before going to war, planting crops or seeking ways to appease the gods for errors they might have made.

During the Roman Empire, observations of natural phenomenon was popular, particularly augury, which studied the reactions of birds and domestic animals during thunder and lightning storms. Romans were also big star gazers and often combined the arrival of celestial meteorites with terrestrial thunder and lightning storms to divine the future (meteoromancy). Romans also had far less inhibitions about the human body than many cultures and often viewed one another naked in the common Roman baths. Perhaps the frequent viewing of naked bodies led to the popular form of divination known as moleosphy, which made predictions based upon moles, birthmarks and skin blemishes.

Greeks and the Oracle of Delphi: One of the most famous paranormal abilities of all time were the cryptic prophecies issued by the Oracle of Delphi in ancient Greece. The location of the Oracle was considered a sacred shrine by Greeks. For most of its history, every kingdom honored the independence of the Oracle grounds, making the shrine available to all Greeks and visitors from other lands. The shrine was built around a fissure in the ground from which issued spring water and an always burning flame of ethylene gas. It was considered by many Greeks to be the sacred center of the world.

Archeologists say that the site of Delphi was inhabited beginning in the 14th century B.C., during the Mycenaean times, by small settlements revolving around the worship of Mother Earth as a deity.

Over the centuries the shrine grew in importance and wealth. As it was only open a few days each year during a nine-month period, and closed for three months every winter, long lines of pilgrims would form weeks before the opening. Wealthy supplicants would donate great treasures and works of art for the privilege of cutting to the head of the line and being graced with an oracle of the future.

The shrine espoused no particular religion and had allegiance to no particular kingdom, though it did have protection of various kings from time to time. Coupled with its geographically central location in Greece, it became a gathering spot for intellectuals and a neutral ground for adversaries to discuss treaties.

By the 8th century BC the Oracle of Delphi had become well-known throughout the countries bordering the Mediterranean Sea and far beyond due to the accurate oracles of the shrine priestesses, particularly one named Pythia. Leaders of almost every kingdom bordering the Mediterranean had absolute faith in the accuracy of Pythia's visions of the future. For many leaders, any major decisions of consequence was only made after consultation with the Oracle of Delphi.

The famous Greek historian Plutarch, was born in a small town only 20 miles from Delphi and for a time served as a priest of the Oracle. It is from his account that we have a description of the inner sanctum and the procedures. Plutarch records that the priestess Pythia would enter a chamber in the inner sanctuary and sit on a tripod that spanned a chasm in the earth from which issued small amounts of hydrocarbon gas (ethylene) which were always burning in flame. Under the mind-altering influence of the gas, Pythia would fall into a trance and begin speaking in a language incomprehensible to mere mortals. Priests such as Plutarch would understand her words and interpret them for the supplicants.

The oracles were famously difficult to decipher, which allowed people to assign their desired meaning to the cryptic words, or assign the ensuing events to coincide with the prophecy, thus insuring a very high accuracy of the oracles. An example of the common dual meaning open to interpretation, would be "You will go you will return not in battle will you perish." Depending on where one adds a single comma the meaning will be exactly opposite. "You will go you will return, not in battle will you perish." Great news! You can go to battle and the Oracle has prophesied that you will not perish but will return home. Or, "You will go you will return not, in battle will you perish." Bad news; you will go away to war but will not return and will perish in battle.

In 356 B.C. The temple grounds were captured by an alliance of Phocians, Athenians and Spartans. Its vast treasures accumulated from supplicants over many centuries, were carted off and sold to finance their war. King Philip of Macedon soon liberated the shrine and it fell under the protection of his victorious empire.

In 191 B.C. the temple was taken over by the Romans and in 86 B.C. it was once again pillaged for its treasures to finance a war. Three years later, now only a shell of its former glory, the temple was thoroughly destroyed by a Thracian named Maedi who is the infamous person that according to legend filled in the fissure and extinguished the sacred flame that had been burning uninterrupted since the memory of man.

Ancient Times: In the more primitive world, any paranormal ability exhibited is likely to have been a significant event and led to the psychics becoming priests, priestesses, shamans and medicine men.

Casting pebbles or bones and predicting the future based upon how they fall and arrange, is a form of divination known as cleromancy that began in very ancient days and continued to be used in related forms through every subsequent era.

Another ancient form of divining that would find no acceptance in the modern world is cephalomancy, which would entailed severing the head of a donkey or goat, then tossing it onto hot coals and making predictions based upon how it burned and smelled.

Interpreting the death throes of living human and animal sacrifices, and studying remnant body parts, seemed to be popular forms of divination in ancient times as well. Extispicy, Haruspication, Hieromancy and Hieroscopy, all which were prophetic techniques based upon the study of the entrails of sacrificed animals. As purchasing animals for sacrifice was beyond the means of common people, they sought their signs of the future by noting the severed heads and entrails of fish (Ichthyomancy).

The Old Testament / Torah dating back over 3,000 years, records Joseph using his psychic abilities to interpret the dreams of the Egyptian Pharaoh. Dream interpretation continued to be a paranormal gift relied upon by kings and leaders through the Greek and Roman times as well, and still holds some fascination with people today.

The Intuition

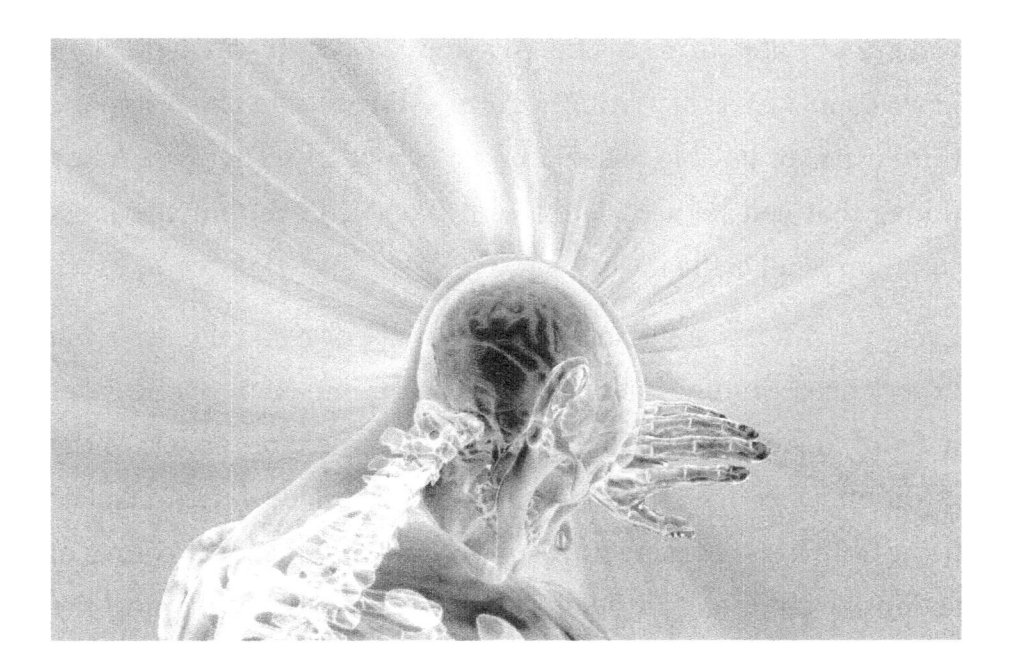

The Third Eye

When it comes to developing the intuition, the number one thing that would be discussed would be the third eye. The third eye is the seat of the intuition. It is the key to the power of clairvoyance, also known as clear seeing. The third eye or Ajna chakra is probably the most common chakra that many people are familiar with. It is what will allow you to see into the world of spirits. Remember that the exact location of the third eye is right between your eyebrows.

The good news is that everyone has a third eye. It is just a matter of developing it, and this is something that you can do. Once you develop your third eye, you will have a powerful intuition, and you will even be able to access the Akashic records. It will depend on how you make use of it. Another interesting reason to develop the third eye is to be able to see prana more clearly. There are many things that can be associated with the third eye, but the most common of all is the intuition.

Every person has some level of intuition. For example, have you experienced simply knowing who is calling your phone even without looking at it? This is a classic example of the use of the intuition. Of course, there are many other practical uses, such as being able to avoid danger or simply knowing the right course of action to take in a difficult situation. Indeed, developing the intuition can be very helpful. Let us now look more into enhancing this natural and psychic ability.

The third eye is also the pineal gland. It is a small endocrine system that regulates the wake-sleep pattern. In spirituality, when you talk about the pineal gland, then you also refer to the third eye.

Activate and Decalcify Your Pineal Gland

The pineal gland or your third eye holds remarkable power. However, only a few people can tap into this power and use it effectively. Many people simply have an underdeveloped third eye. But the good news is that there are exercises that you can do to strengthen your third eye so you can start using and enjoying its immense power. Let us discuss them one by one:

- Who is it?

This is something that you can do every time your phone rings or beeps. Simply ask yourself, "Who is it?" Pay attention to what you see in your mind's eye. Do you see any image or impressions? Be open to receiving messages. This is how you can connect to your intuition. You should also realize that you have a strong intuition and that you only have to learn to connect to it. Of course, this technique is not limited to calls or texts on your phone. You can also adjust it a bit and use it in other ways. For example, if you hear a knock or any sound at night, you can ask, "What is it?" and pay attention to any messages that you get from your intuition. The important thing is to start connecting to your intuition once again.

- Forehead press

This technique is becoming popular these days. This, however, does not work on everyone but it is still worth trying. This will allow you some specks of prana in the air. They usually appear as little dots or any form of white light. The steps are as follows:

Place your index finger in the area between the eyebrows where the Ajna chakra is. Press it gently and maintain pressure for about 50 seconds. Slowly remove your finger, blink your eyes around five times, and look at a blank wall. Just focus lightly and try to see with your peripheral vision. Do you see little dots or any specks of white light? This is prana in the air.

To help you see the energy, you might want to do this in a dimly lit room. Look at a wall with a neutral background. This is a good way to use your third eye to see energy, but it is not a recommended method to strengthen the Ajna chakra. Still, this is something that is worth trying, especially if you just want to see prana.

- Visual screen

This is a good technique to use for visualization exercises. To locate the visual screen, close your eyes and look slightly upward. With eyes closed, look at the area of the Ajna chakra. This is your visual screen. You can project anything that you like to this screen, especially images. You can consider this as some form of internal magic mirror.

The main purpose of this visual screen is for your visualization exercises. Here is a simple exercise you can do to increase your concentration and willpower:

Assume a meditative posture and relax. Now, look at your visual screen. Imagine an apple floating in front of you. Now, just focus on this apple and do not entertain any other thoughts. This is just like the breathing meditation. However, instead of focusing on your breath, focus on the apple in your visual screen.

When you are ready to end this meditation, simply visualized the apple slowly fade away and gently open your eyes.

You are also welcome to use any other object for this meditation. If you do not want to use an apple, you can visualize an orange or even an elephant. The important thing is to have a point of visual focus for this meditation.

- Charging with the fire element

Remember that the intuition is associated with the pineal gland, in the pineal gland is the third eye chakra. Now, this third eye chakra is associated with the fire element. Therefore, you can empower your third eye chakra by charging it with the element of fire. This is a powerful technique so be sure to use it carefully. The steps are as follows:

Assume a meditative posture and relax. Close your eyes. Now, visualize the brilliant and powerful sun above you. This powerful sun is full of the element of fire. As you inhale, see and feel that you are drawing the energy from the sun. Let the energy charge your third eye chakra and empower it. Do this with every inhalation. The more that you charge your third eye, the more that it lights up and become more powerful. Have faith that with every inhalation, you become more and more intuitive.

Keep in mind that this is a powerful technique. If you are just starting out, it is suggested that you only do up to 10 inhalations in the beginning. You can then add one or two more inhalations every week. You will know if you can execute this technique properly because you will feel pressure on your forehead in the area of your third eye chakra. Take note that you should not just visualize your third eye chakra getting stronger, but you should also be conscious that your intuition becomes more powerful the more that you charge your third eye. The power of visualization should be accompanied by your intention.

Note

It should be noted that the Ajna chakra and crown chakra are closely connected. If you want to improve your intuition, it is only right that you also work on your crown chakra. Of course, this does not mean that you should ignore your other chakras. Again, the whole chakra system is important to your spiritual development and to the awakening of the kundalini.

The Language Of Divination

Perhaps the most fascinating psychic tradition is that of divination. Different forms of divination have been in use from prehistoric times to the modern day, involving everything from animal sacrifice to the reading of everyday playing cards. Needless to say, some of these forms are not everyone's idea of a good time. That is assuming you aren't the type of person who would be willing to sacrifice a goat just to know whether or not you should ask someone out on a date! However, most forms of divination are far less extreme, requiring nothing more than a deck of cards, a canister of sticks, or a bag of tiles. These forms allow the average psychic the opportunity to tap into their subconscious and gain insights that would otherwise be beyond reach. In fact, divination can be seen as the waking form of dreaming in the respect that it allows the practitioner the opportunity to access deeper levels of knowledge much like a psychic dream. Additionally, many of the 'languages' of different divination tools are very symbolic, reflecting the language of psychic dreams.

There are far too many types of divination to cover in such a short space, so this chapter will focus on four of the main forms used in the modern day. These forms cover two basic variations of divination—single question divination and big picture divination. Single question divination covers the forms that usually produce a single reading, meaning that they are intended to convey the possible outcome of a particular course of action. These usually involve such questions as "What will be the outcome if I accept this job offer?" or "How will my date with so and so go tonight?" Big picture divination is a more complex form of divination, given to exploring the dynamics of a situation. These forms often produce detailed readings involving numerous cards, tiles or other devices. Readers of big picture divination will often get insights into energies working for them, energies working against them, and several choices that the reader must make. These forms of divination usually require a great deal of study in order to master, and they require the utmost of concentration and devotion in order to use properly.

The first type of divination to explore is that of single question divination. While there are various forms of this practice perhaps the two most well-known and commonly used are the I Ching and Chinese fortune sticks. Both of these forms of divination come from Ancient China, and they serve as a testament to the mindset of the Ancient Chinese. The average person in Ancient China believed that the gods were there to help guide them in making the right choices at any given time. This meant that the spirit realm was an extension of the physical realm, not something to be feared or worshipped. Subsequently, the divine forces were there for everyone, regardless of status. To do a reading in I Ching or fortune sticks was to virtually ask the gods for advice. The fact that these divination forms exist to this day suggests that this outlook on the spirit realm is very much alive and well in modern times.

In the case of the I Ching there are 64 hexagrams, or sets of six-line readings. Each hexagram represented a story or legend from Ancient China, one which conveys a lesson or a message. To determine which hexagram was relevant the reader would cast three coins six different times. These coins would land heads up or tails up, and the reader would use this to determine each of the six lines. After the sixth cast was complete the full hexagram would be revealed. The reader would then turn to the appropriate hexagram in the book for the message revealed. This practice was used in other Asian cultures as well as China, and in fact it is reported that the Imperial Japanese Navy used the I Ching prior to the attack on Pearl Harbor in 1941. The fact that such significant decisions were based on psychic readings demonstrates how much faith the Eastern cultures place on divination and its ability to provide direction and wisdom.

The second form of divination used for single question situations are Chinese fortune sticks. There are several variations on this theme, however the most commonly used format also provides 64 different readings. Unlike the I Ching, which requires six different castings of three coins, the fortune sticks require only one casting. In this scenario the reader has a canister with 64 separate sticks, each numbered accordingly. The reader will shake the canister in a way that will make the sticks slowly emerge. This process will be performed until a single stick leaves the canister and lands on the table or the floor, depending on where the reading is being performed. Once the stick is identified the reader will turn to the appropriate number in the book that contains the fortune stick readings. Like the I Ching, this book contains different stories and fables from Ancient China, each with a unique message and subsequent advice. Sometimes two or three sticks will fall out at once, and in this instance the reader must make a choice. Many people choose to treat all of the fallen sticks as significant and read all of the readings that they convey. Others choose to put the sticks back in the canister and do it again until only one falls out. In the end, there is no real right or wrong answer. The trick is to do what is right for you.

Single question divination is an excellent way to try to answer a pressing question in the moment. For the most part these readings allow the reader to decide whether or not they should pursue a certain course of action. There are times, however, when a more in-depth understanding of a situation is required. For these events big picture divination is a better source for answers. Just as with single question divination, big picture divination has many forms. Again, there are far too many to cover in the limited space available here. Therefore we will examine two of the most commonly used forms in existence today—Tarot and Runes. These forms of divination have origins that go back into history, although they aren't necessarily as old as the Chinese forms we have examined.

In the case of Tarot cards, the earliest known Tarot deck goes back to the middle of the 1400s. The purpose of the original Tarot cards was not for divination, rather they were actual playing cards much like our modern playing cards, containing different suits and numerical values. However, as time progressed, the rich symbolism of these cards attracted mystics who were looking for a medium for discovering wisdom and deep insight. Eventually a system was devised which gave each card a specific symbolic value, meaning that the Tarot deck became a way to tap into the wisdom of the subconscious. A great many spreads became available, meaning that any number of situations could be contemplated using the cards. There are 11 such spreads commonly used today, ranging from the single card spread which allows the reader to gain insight on a single question, much as with fortune sticks or the I Ching, to spreads of as many as eight or more cards. A spread of three cards allows the reader to gain insight on the progression of a situation by revealing the past, present and future. Other spreads provide deeper revelations, including energies that stand in favor of the situation, those that oppose the situation, and even lessons that the reader needs to learn from the situation at hand. The standard Tarot deck consists of 78 cards, meaning that there is an endless source of wisdom and insight available to the reader.

One of the wonderful things about the Tarot deck is that it has gone through numerous changes over the years. The earliest and most original of the decks are still available today, but other decks with different imagery are also available, meaning that the reader can choose a deck that best reflects their personality. Additionally, different decks can be used to better represent the specific situation at hand. While this may seem fairly superficial at first it actually represents a very critical element of divination—the connection between the reader and the source of the wisdom. Whether you believe that divination is a way to communicate to the divine, or whether you believe it is merely a way to tap into your own subconscious (there are those who would argue one's subconscious is divine), the important thing is that the medium represent your personal vision of that which you are accessing. Therefore, different imagery options allow a person to find the imagery that best captures their vision of the source that the information will be coming from. This personalization makes the experience all the more meaningful, as it makes the reader a more integral part of the process.

Finally, there is the divination tool known as Runes. Like Tarot cards, Runes were originally not designed for use as a divination tool. Rather, Runes were the characters of the original Germanic alphabet used by the Scandinavian and Germanic cultures in the era commonly referred to as the Dark Ages—a thousand-year timeframe beginning in the 5th century and ending in the 15th century. Different variations of Runes emerged across the different Germanic cultures, but the version that is used for divinatory purposes is the one knows as Futhark Runes. Specifically known as the Elder Futhark, this group consists of 24 different Runes, each with a phonetic and symbolic value. The name Futhark itself comes from the phonetic value of the first six Runes, Fehu, Uruz, Thurisaz, Ansuz, Raidho and Kenaz. The first letters of each Rune combine to form the name, just as the first two letters of the Greek alphabet are used to form the word alphabet—alpha and beta. While the Runes were originally just the alphabet of the Germanic or Teutonic peoples, they became a tool of divination that is unsurpassed in symbolism and rich imagery.

Unlike Chinese divination, which uses poetry, legends and stories to convey wisdom, Runes use more primal images in their language. Uruz, for example, represents the Auroch, a wild bison that covered Northern Europe in prehistoric times. This Rune symbolizes the raw strength and power of the Auroch, therefore when a reader draws Uruz they are inspired by the promise of strength that it portends. Thurisaz is the Rune for thorn, and it represents the barriers that thorns can be. In the case where a reader draws this Rune, they are cautioned that the road ahead may be full of challenges, much like the rose bush is full of thorns. Certain pains will be experienced in the course of achieving the goal. The simplicity and primal quality of Rune symbolism makes it a favorite for anyone who embraces a more shamanic relationship with the divine side of life.

Runes can be read using the same 11 spreads as is used with Tarot readings. A single Rune can give insight into a single question, whereas a three Rune reading can give insight into the progression of a situation. Other readings can indicate a fork in the road, where choices have to be made, or they can indicate the forces working for and against the reader in a particular situation. In the end, even though there are only 24 Runes as opposed to the 78 cards of a Tarot deck, there is still a virtually limitless number of readings that can come from a Rune session. The fact that there are fewer Runes makes this the oracle of choice for anyone who prefers a simpler, less complicated divination tool. That said, the simplicity of the Runes should not be cause to underestimate their true value. The truth of the matter is that Runes are perhaps the most symbolic of the divination forms discussed in this chapter. Rather than drawing on intricate imagery or written wisdom, Runes employ basic symbols to tap into the subconscious mind. In a way, Runes are virtually dream symbolism in waking life. To do a Rune cast is to essentially have a psychic dream with your eyes wide open.

Another benefit of Runes over other forms of divination is the level of personalization that can be achieved with them. Chinese divination is relatively fixed, in that the only real way the reader can personalize the experience is to have a unique interpretation of the wisdom or advice revealed. While Tarot cards offer more opportunities for personalization through the use of different imagery this is the limit of their flexibility. Runes, however, allow the reader to bring personalization to both the form of the Runes and the meanings they possess. In terms of form, since there are only 24 Runes and the symbols are very basic, including the X of Gebo, the R of Raidho, and the H of Hagalaz, any person can create their own set of Runes without much difficulty. Variations of Rune sets include printed cards, painted stones, and even scorched wood. Anyone with even the most modest of artistic skills can create a wonderful set of Runes, thus bringing the reader into the very heart of the medium itself. A set of Runes created by the reader is said to be infinitely more powerful than a set purchased in a shop as it contains the very heart and soul of the reader.

The symbolic meaning of the Runes can take on a personal aspect as well. This is due to the primitive nature of the symbolism involved. For example, the rune Dagaz, which means daybreak, can come to mean several different things. For one person the Rune can represent the dawn after the darkness, an end of bad times and a beginning of better times. For another it might indicate the beginning of a project or of a new chapter of life. For yet another reader it might indicate the speed with which change will be experienced. Daybreak is pretty immediate, unlike the year cycle represented by the Rune Jera. Therefore, while each Rune has a basic meaning that is essential to its understanding, any number of personal embellishments can be added to the meaning, just as they can be added onto the form of the Rune itself. This is particularly important for anyone who seeks to embark on a journey of self-discovery. As Rune readings begin to take on specific meanings for that person then they can create their own version of Rune interpretation. In essence, Runes can become the very personal and intimate language spoken between the reader and the divine source of wisdom that the Runes tap into.

Whether a person chooses to use traditional forms of divination, such as the I Ching or fortune sticks, or whether they choose other methods such as Tarot cards or Runes, the important thing is that the practitioner chooses the method that works best for them. At some point a person will know whether a particular tool resonates with them or whether it feels cold and distant. What is critical is that a person feels connected to the source of wisdom when using their chosen form of divination. Divination is a spiritual experience, a connection between the reader and the divine. Therefore, it should be a special occasion each and every time it is practiced. Rather than seeing the divination tool as a tile, a stick or a piece of writing the reader should see it as the words spoken to them by the very mouth of the universe itself.

The First Step To Developing Your Psychic Power

Before you can become a psychic, it is important that you learn first to clear your psyche. Psychic awakening can be difficult since the psychic concept itself is often misunderstood. Therefore, you must make an effort and take your time in clearing your mind as well as letting go of your old patterns.

An unclear psyche will take your energy away. This will prevent you from raising your consciousness. Most people have a linear perspective. With this kind of thinking, you limit yourself. A limited perspective will prevent you from realizing and developing your psychic abilities.

You have to open yourself up to growth. Growth will give way to enlightenment. If you refuse to grow, you remain closed and unable to enhance your innate psychic abilities.

Clearing your psyche means altering your negative thought patterns. When you are successful at this, you become more open to spiritual lessons. Welcoming these spiritual lessons is very important in becoming a pure psychic. So, how do you exactly achieve clearance?

Acknowledge the Negative Trait

The first thing you must do is to acknowledge the presence of the negative trait. You cannot deal with it successfully if you are not willing to admit or acknowledge its presence.

Think about what can hold you back from growing and transcending. It could be an event or a certain issue in your life. Examine it carefully. Look at it from every angle. Ask yourself why you are bothered by this issue. Think about how it affects you.

Set the Form

After defining the issue, the next step is to give it a form. Start by picking a spot where you can put your mind in a meditative state. With your mind at ease and free from distraction, focus on the issue. Imagine the issue and allow images to take form. You have to be in and with it.

Forgive

Now, you must forgive. First, you have to forgive yourself for being bothered by this issue. You also need to forgive other people who may be involved in the issue. You cannot release yourself from this issue unless you forgive and completely let go.

While in a meditative state, visualize yourself asking for forgiveness. Visualize yourself forgiving.

Let Go

You cannot force the issue out of your mind unless you have forgiven. During your meditation, visualize yourself opening the door so you can let the issue out, as well as the people who may play a part in it. Visualize the issue going out. Watch it as it floats and fades away. Once you do this, you will feel overwhelmed with forgiveness and unconditional love. You will feel lighter, as if a huge burden has been lifted from your heart and from your entire being.

Negativity can only work to stop you from achieving your full psychic potential. This is why it is very important for you to learn to accept, release, and move forward, unburdening yourself from negative issues and thoughts, especially those involving other people.

Once you have let go of your baggage, you are in a better position to develop your psychic ability. The next step involves accepting or acknowledging the existence of that ability.

Acknowledge Your Psychic Ability

It is quite impossible to develop or nourish something without having first accepted its existence. In this step, it is recommended that you first work on getting a better understanding of what you are dealing with.

You can read articles or refer to psychic accounts as well as learn from biographies. When you read about other people's experiences, it can become clearer that what is happening to you is normal. It has happened to other people, too. This will also help you become more aware and conscious of the things that come to you as a result of the awakening.

What Happens When You Fail to Acknowledge Your Ability?

We have gone over the reasons why you should develop your extraordinary skills. Now, you may wonder what will happen if you suppress it rather than embrace it, as most people choose to do the former. Below is a list of the most common symptoms.

Headaches

We have mentioned earlier that headaches can be experienced in the process of psychic awakening. Headaches occur because of the influx of energy, which usually happens during the awakening process.

But resistance can also bring about headaches. In fact, aches may not only be felt in the head. It is common to feel physical pain all over the body.

Your chakras, or energy centers, are starting to open up as well as your senses, from which the body receives psychic information. When you try to shut down your ability, you force these chakras to close, and that can result in a physical tightening.

Lack of Sleep

When you ignore the signs of awakening and dismiss your psychic abilities, you are bound to feel the consequences of such suppression physically. In fact, you may also start losing sleep. As you postpone acknowledging your ability, you prevent yourself from developing and learning how to control information as you receive it.

During awakening, you can become physically sensitive. The more you try to shut down your ability, the more it forces itself upon you. You may be able to resist it in a conscious state. However, suppressing your ability or pieces of psychic information can become much more challenging in the sleep state, when you are more receptive.

In addition to depriving yourself of deep sleep, you are also bound to experience repetitive nightmares. The sooner you acknowledge the psychic information that comes to you, the earlier you can learn how to control it. That means you will find it much easier to relieve yourself from the discomfort.

Disconnected

It is completely natural for you to feel uncomfortable with the psychic information that is coming to you. Being uncomfortable and deliberately ignoring and dismissing it, however, are two different things.

Because a lot of information seems to find its way to you and you choose to disregard it anyway, you will feel disconnected. Psychic information comes more frequently when you are surrounded by people. In an effort to shut out the psychic ability, a person tends to isolate him or herself.

Surely, this is not a measure that you would want to take—that is, to be left alone. It may be difficult to deal with something you cannot fully explain, but it is more difficult to live life in isolation.

Depression

In an effort to deny your innate psychic ability, it is also possible that you will fall into a state of depression. By denying your gift, you deny a part of yourself.

As soon as you accept this side of you and acknowledge that you have received a special gift, you become able to achieve a more balanced life, especially when it comes to dealing with psychic information as you receive it. This gift cannot be forced. It manifests itself, and when it happens, you have to choose which way to go.

Protecting Yourself Against Spirits

When you have psychic abilities, you have to learn how to protect yourself, your life, and your loved ones from spirits. I have discussed how there are spirits out there who want to do nothing but bring chaos and turmoil to your life. You have to look at it like this if there are good spirits than there has to be bad spirits. There could not be one without the other. So, when you are trying to contact the good spirits you open yourself up to the bad ones too.

You see, all spirits are attracted to you because they know they can communicate with you. You give off a sort of light in the spirit world. It is when bad spirits take notice of this light that you have to be careful. You see, each of these spirits has a different purpose, they all come to cause problems in your life but they cause different types of problems.

When you first realize that a bad spirit has gotten close to you it may be something like a creepy feeling, your hair may stand up on the back of your neck or on your arms. You just get the feeling of uneasiness. If this is left unchecked, the spirit will only grow stronger. Usually it will start to show itself in dark places, you may see a darker than dark spot in the corner of your house. You may see something run by out of the corner of your eye, or you may just get the feeling that you are being watched. If you allow it to get this far, you must take action at this point or it will only get worse. I will discuss with you what to do later in the chapter.

If you continue to allow the spirit in your life, you may be awoken at night to strange noises or the feeling that someone is standing over your bed. There are times that you will actually be able to see a figure depending on how strong the spirit is at this point. Blankets may get pulled off of you while you are sleeping or you may feel like someone has touched you.

Both of these have happened to me. The first occurrence was when my blankets were literally pulled off of me. I was visiting my mother for the week and pregnant with my daughter. My son and I were sleeping on my mother's couches in her living room at the time. We had gone to bed and been asleep for a while when I felt a tug at my blanket. Not thinking I said to my son to go back to sleep, pulled the blanket back up on me and started to go back to sleep. I felt an uneasiness and looked to see where my son was. He was sound asleep on the other couch. He hadn't moved since I put him to bed. I rolled over and started to go back to sleep when it happened again, this time it was much harder. I jerked the blanket back up on me trying to ignore what was trying to get my attention when the blanket was literally ripped out of my hands and thrown across the room.

Not having lived in that house, I had no idea what was going on. I was terrified because my mother had told me stories about how people were said to have changed once they moved out to that property. I left the house that night without saying a word, I packed up my son and went to a hotel. The next day I decided to do some research and found out that the property was on the trail of tears. Now I am not saying that the Cherokee are out there pulling blankets off of people, what I am saying is there was a lot of anger and sorrow that happened in that area and evil feeds off of that. Whatever it was that was taunting me that night was not a friendly Cherokee Chief. It was something much much worse.

The second thing that occurred was once again when I was pregnant with my daughter. I was asleep in my bed at my apartment and had been upset because the anniversary of my Grandfathers passing was approaching. I had been experiencing a lot of different activity at the apartment and my neighbors had also. So, I was well aware of what was going on there. People were being tormented daily because one of the neighbors had released an evil spirit through a séance. Anyway, as I was asleep in my bed, I got the feeling that something was in the room with me. As you all know, you get a different kind of feeling when there is something with you that wants to cause you harm. I felt my blanket be lifted from my foot and whatever it was grabbed one of my toes and shook it. This was not a friendly hey wake up kind of thing. This was a HEY I am here and you are not going to ignore me kind of thing.

I didn't deal with the spirit at the time and it continued to get stronger through the years. There came a point that I thought if I left the apartment everything would go back to normal but that was not the case. It went with me to my new place because it loved taunting me and my son so much. I ended up having to clean it from my house and it moved into an old shed in the neighborhood. It left me alone when it found others to taunt.

Because I didn't have a lot of money at the time, I didn't live in a very great neighborhood. It was full of drunks, drug addicts, and people who were sleeping around with a different person every night. The spirit felt right at home. I saw it again just one time, it looked out of the shed as I was walking my dog, almost as if to say can I come back but I was very stern with it and told it never again.

So, what do you do if you come across a spirit like this that wants nothing more than to cause you harm? Well as I said earlier, the sooner you deal with it the better off you will be. The longer you let it go, the stronger it will get. If you get it early it will be weak and you will not have to fight very hard to get it to go.

One thing you can do if you want to get a bad spirit out of your life is to focus on your religious beliefs. Most of us believe in something and it is that belief that will help you get through something like this. Personally, I believe in God. I believe in the Bible and I put those beliefs into action. So, when the spirit was in my home that is exactly what I did.

You need to make sure all of your children are out of the house before you attempt to rid yourself or your home from any type of spirit. You also need to ensure there is no one present who has weak faith. These people are easy for spirits to take over and you do not want to be responsible for that.

You also need to know what your strengths are. For me that is singing. I love to sing and it makes me feel strong and close to God. Then you need to get your faith involved. Whatever it is that your faith says you need to do to rid yourself of evil is what you will do.

This is what I did. I got some Holy Oil from my church and sent my children to my mother's house. I then spent the day cleaning because I knew the spirit preferred to show itself at night. While I was cleaning, I was searching for were the spirit was hiding which turned out to be in a back bedroom at the far end of the house. I also spent the day singing hymns and songs I remembered from church. This made me feel like I was strong enough to take anything on.

At 10 O'clock that night I felt the spirit becoming very strong. I began by blessing all the doors and windows in my home. I blessed my children's beds and everything in their bedrooms. I sat myself down facing the hallway which lead to the bedroom it had been hiding and began to sing. I sang for over an hour before I began to get a reaction. That is when I saw the spirit for the first time.

He was very large and he was standing at the entrance of the hallway. I began screaming at him to get out of my home and to leave me and my family alone. When I felt like I was becoming weak I would begin singing then scream at him some more. This went on until 2 am but I knew as long as I didn't give up, he would have to leave. Then I realized he had to have a way to leave. I opened my front door and yelled at him to get out.

There was a rush of wind that went by me and he was gone. I have never had to deal with this spirit again and I can honestly say that I never want to.

If you are dealing with such a spirit it is imperative that you have a strong faith in something larger than yourself. Like I said, for me that is God. I knew he would protect me from such a spirit and it was my faith in what the Bible says that got me through. You must have some type of faith in order to overcome these types of spirits.

Prepare yourself ahead of time for what you are going to face. I did so by watching as many exorcism videos as possible. As cliché as that may seem, I wanted to see what would happen if worst came to worst. I did this for a few days before I felt like I was prepared to take this spirit on. I also read all the information I could on demons. I did this because it is my belief that if a spirit is not good and is therefore evil, it is a demon. I wanted to know everything I could about what I was going to face. I also prayed a lot. I prayed for protection on me and my children. I prayed that if I had done something to bring this spirit into my home that I be forgiven of it.

It took me about 4 days of preparation before I knew I was ready to face the demon. I suggest that you take all the time you need to prepare yourself because if you face an evil spirit unprepared, it will take over your body and you will have no control of it after that. You will just be a vessel for the spirit to use when and how it wants to.

If you face a spirit like this, do not fear, do not feel as if you cannot handle it, have faith in yourself that you can concur it. If you end up without hope and feeling like you just cannot do it on your own, find someone who has more experience in dealing with evil spirits. There are many people out there who have gone through what you are going through and they are more than willing to help you.

Conclusion

Psychic abilities are no longer the superstitions that people whisper about in the shadows. These powers are not possessed or used for evil and not for just speaking to people that have crossed over. As you have learned, psychic abilities are available to all at birth. These abilities are born in your frontal lobe, growing or dying depending on childhood experiences or support from family members early in life. Depending on your childhood, you may find as you practice these exercises that psychic abilities come naturally to you because you have been able to practice and experience these powers from a very young age. Others will find that, although it may feel different at first, psychic abilities are not impossible to achieve. Through intense concentration and continued practice, one can gain the ability to open their mind and allow energy to flow in.

By using any of the foundational meditation exercises, you learn that the core of mastering your psychic abilities is able to still your mind, body, and soul. Centering yourself makes it possible to open your mind to the vibrations of energy within the environment. The three different meditation exercises, traditional meditation, bright light meditation and chakra meditation, all focus on one goal, which is to empty your mind and allow your abilities to reveal themselves. This is the first step to discovering your psychic abilities.

Once you have mastered the meditation exercises, you have the ability to practice many different forms of psychic powers. One form may come more naturally to you. Once you find your natural form of psychic abilities, you should embrace that and continue to practice and master the form. Psychics are typically specialists in one or two forms of psychic powers. It is important to practice all the forms several times in order to find the ability that your mind was meant to perform. You can use this form of psychic powers to enhance your life, bring you closer to people in your life, connect with your body and open yourself to the universe around you in order to feel peace and happiness every day of your life.

Made in the USA
Coppell, TX
15 May 2020